Through the Anarchist Press

for Leah

many years later

John Rety

2/4/2006

Through the Anarchist Press
– a column in Freedom

John Rety

with drawings
by
Emily Johns

FREEDOM PRESS
London
1996

First published
by
FREEDOM PRESS
84b Whitechapel High Street
London
E1 7QX
1996

ISBN 0 900384 85 9

Cover illustration of 'Greenham Common Regained' by Emily Johns

Typeset by Jayne Clementson

Printed in Great Britain by Aldgate Press, London E1 7RQ

It was at the annual Freedom Bookshop party when it occurred to me that it was a good time to think about new year resolutions. It was probably the good company and sparkling conversations which induced the thought, although I have been thinking about it for some time previously, that I shall stop reading any other than anarchist literature, that is newspapers and periodicals, for the coming year and that I shall experiment relying entirely on news percolating through the anarchist press. In other words, I will not bother my head with the news unless I read it in *Freedom*. I am one of those rare people who haven't got a television set and only turn on the radio to listen to the weather forecast, and although people around me listen to the radio all day long, I would be more interested to tune in if it *was* a pirate broadcast.

There is nothing much I can do about seeing the headlines as I walk around town, but I shall try to avert my eyes as much as possible. Should Major resign, I would wait to be officially informed until *Freedom* deigns to announce the great news, although come to think of it Harold Wilson could still be prime minister for I cannot remember *Freedom* ever having disclosed to us that he wasn't.

I hope people won't accuse me of becoming parochial, for the news that is dished out in the national press is already tendentious stuff and as long as it has not become compulsory to read their wretched propaganda I shall not be sent to a place of correction.

But that is as may be. For I am reliably informed that the law- making industry has never been so busy, that ministers now first commit atrocities then have a law passed to make their action legal and even if it is played according to old Erskine May (look it up) these gangsters can push through their government by decree in less than a day.

It was good to meet so many anarchists crowding out Freedom Press, and of course I made my pilgrimage to Arthur Moyse's court where I was reliably informed that our esteemed art correspondent had not missed a Saturday yet in twenty years. Again there is no better table talk in London.

I hope I can keep this up for a year, even to the extent that if there was going to be an anarchist revolution in this country I shall only believe it if I see it printed in *Freedom*.

8th January 1994

It is easy for people who live in big cities and scarcely leave their boundaries to forget that there is another life outside the walls.

Perhaps only anarchists notice this qualitative difference, that the further you find yourself from the centre the less is the consistent power of the state.

Here on this Scottish island nobody reads the papers. Should the government resign tomorrow, nobody would toss a caber.

The whole island (this time of year – in summer when the tourists arrive in their coaches it is different) goes about its business without any of the nightmarish burdens the close vicinity of government produces in the people.

No police, no ambulances, no fire engines, no cop cars racing about. On the contrary, front doors are left open. People call on each other, you can return to your home full of visitors. Somebody is blowing a bagpipe in the kitchen – who he is and how he got there nobody knows. A bit of a contrast with the big city where powerful lights go on if you stop for a second in front of somebody's precious front garden.

People here display a common courtesy for each other, an innate sympathy that makes you not want to return to the big city. The air in your lungs is worth all the chemist's prescriptions. At night you can actually see the stars. The big city is a bad smell in your memory. Its broken down system, its purposeless noise, authorities' heavy hand cannot be imagined here.

"All of us are born equal, none of us are born to be slaves" – the old revolutionary slogan had some meaning here.

You mention the town you come from and people look at you pityingly. "I can't imagine living there, not me thank you", they say, not in that conurbation of many millions breathing in the exhaust fumes of its filthy air. Its poor children, a great proportion of its good people in useless jobs or on the dole, its mean rich leading their futile lives behind the barbed wire of their 'security'.

"[But] here's a hand, my trusty fiere,
And gies a hand o' thine;
And we'll tak a cup o' kindness yet,
For auld lang syne!"

I walk down to the harbour, Robert Burns's song ringing in my ears, there is an eerie light over the black hills and the lights of a nearby island glow in the distance.

Waiting for a coach connection in Glasgow, I wandered down

Sauchihall Street and into the excellent Centre for Community Arts (surely a place where a copy of *Freedom* or *The Raven* would look good on the shelves) where I had the chance to look at one of the best photographic exhibitions I have seen for a long time. The photographer Owen Logan, being a Glasgow Italian, took as his subject the life of exiles.

The central focus concerned the sinking of the SS Arandora Star. The story is worth re-telling for in its brutality it rivals the Belgrano. When Italy entered the war on 10th June 1940, within hours the Glasgow Italians (no doubt many anarchists among them) were rounded up, their dwellings and workplaces looted and set on fire and many of the men were detained and interned prior to their deportation to Canada. The Arandora Star carrying these men left Liverpool for Canada and was torpedoed by a German submarine with a loss of 700 men. After fifty years this dreadful incident is not forgotten by the descendants. One of the most poignant photographs depicts just a hand holding a snapshot of a relation who perished at sea. The story is told of one of the remaining Italian organ-grinders who, to avoid the ire of the crowd, pinned a notice on his barrel-organ: "I'm British and the monkey is from India".

22nd January 1994

Readers may remember a new year resolution of mine that I would endeavour for a year not to read anything else but the anarchist press and see whether by the end of the year I shall be any wiser. I have kept to this resolution, which has resulted in two unforeseen boons – one that I had a lot of extra time reading books, and the other that I have been able to concentrate a bit better on anarchist matters raised in *Freedom* and in other vital periodicals.

One book which I had at last finished reading and enjoyed immensely is *Tristram Shandy*, which I would recommend to comrades to while away the time as they are manning barricades or worse. Another author whom I found soporific is Thomas Quincey, whose great wish was "if I were dug up two centuries hence, I should be found a perfect specimen of a fossil Tory" and I found this to be a true prophecy. He is best when he quotes others such as "*Gaudensque viam fecisse ruina*" (referring to our rulers, no doubt, to a race of man of furious destroyers exulting in the desolation they spread).

Asbestos is in the underground, read all about it, I found documented in a scholarly work by Ellis Hillman in his *London Under London: a subterranean guide* (John Murray, 1993) which is full of interesting snippets on London's lost rivers, its decaying sewers and other such wonders. But clearly the bit of news which ought to become a screaming headline in newspapers I will not see, on which questions will be asked in Parliament and will become a source of much television drama and perhaps will result in a demand for the shutting down of the whole system of London Underground transport until the situation is remedied, is contained in the following comment brazenly printed on page 129 of the aforementioned book: "London Underground at night can be a terrifying place, especially if we were to encounter what London Transport night crews call the 'Asbestos Train', which resembles a vast vacuum-operated snow-plough and travels very slowly – less than a mile an hour – through the tunnels sucking up rubbish. Officially that is its only function. It does have another role, however. For over fifty years London Transport's engine brakes have been lined with asbestos. The asbestos content of the brake lining is less than five per cent, but each time a brake is applied tiny particles of asbestos are released into the atmosphere. Over the years a film has built up on the tunnel lining which, each time the air is disturbed by a train, is blown from the walls into the faces of the passengers waiting on the platforms. Soon a new Swedish brake lining which does not use asbestos will be available, but for some years yet the systematic vacuuming of the tunnels – removing the asbestos along with the rubbish – must go on, preferably at night *when as few people as possible know about it"*. Such is the paternalistic society we live in today. I can but print this and wait patiently for an anarchist society. In the meantime, any comment?

I had a letter from the indefatigable Ian Bone who is organising Anarchy in the UK '94, reminding me of a conversation we had at the anarchist bookfair about my being, strictly speaking, still the acting secretary of that august body the Anarchist Federation of Britain. As there is talk of its revival at the moment, he has asked me and I have agreed to initiate a debate within the Anarchy in the UK event. On the other point that I should contact interested parties, I feel this is outside the duties of an *acting* secretary who is no more than a letter- box, until such time as the Federation is revived and becomes a functioning body. Personally I have an open mind on this subject. Clearly the AFB was needed in the '60s because of the numerous anarchist groups which sprouted at about that time.

The provisional programme for Anarchy in the UK October 21st to 30th events in London is due out by 1st March and is available from PO Box 96, Bristol BS99 1BW (s.a.e. plus £1). It will be interesting to see how much 'mutual aid' will be offered to Ian Bone in his single-handed effort to 'shake the world in ten days'.

Which leads us to yet another quote, this time from Hugh McDiarmid: "What happens to us / Is irrelevant to the world's geology / But what happens to the world's geology / Is not irrelevant to us."

5th February 1994

"Those who are successful become successful by refraining to offend the multitude by favouring the few", said Tacitus. On other pages he refers to the power of eloquence which brings untold wealth to those who possess the gift of blarney. He understood how mean and nasty people could become rich by their use of oratory. Tacitus would not have been surprised by the accumulated wealth and arrogance of the present-day orators in assemblies, law courts and shareholders' meetings, however he would rue the lack of standards in the delivery.

His dialogue on oratory, from which the excerpt was taken, is written in simple language and in parts sounds like a present-day *Freedom* editorial: urbane, witty and devastating. That we have a copy to read is remarkable in itself, for this most important work by Tacitus, written in the first century, 'went out of public view' for thirteen centuries. The first trace of the existence of such a manuscript occurs in 1425 when we find the antiquarian Poggio rejoicing in the offer that had been made to him by a Hersfeld monk offering him for sale a codex containing *aliqua opera Cornelli Taciti nobis* (certain works of Tacitus unknown to us). Poggio hung about in Rome, but the monk did not come across with the manuscript. Nevertheless, secular knowledge soon had to follow, even if Poggio died before it happened. What is remarkable is how fortunate we are that his book survives for us; in company with many other authors like Properitus, Tacitus was as if he had never existed for over a thousand years. But then, of course, nobody had seen the manuscript Poggio was offered. When the Vatican got hold of the copy it allowed further copies to be made, but the 'original' has disappeared from public view.

Sometimes I wonder how such a repressive system has come about which can make a thing of common treasury disappear for a thousand years.

George Orwell was a deft hand at this type of thing in a modern setting, where history changes at the push of a button. I have just come across his unpublished war diaries, excerpts of which were printed in *World Review* (June 1950). In the words of the editor Stefan Schimanski, "we have thinned the manuscript ..." partly to omit certain speculations which have since been superseded by our knowledge of the course of events.

Orwell comes through in these war diaries as fussy, irritable and slightly dotty. He wants to be a soldier again ...

"26th June 1940: Horribly depressed by the way things are turning out. Went this morning for my Medical Board and was turned down, my grade being C. What is appalling is the unimaginativeness of a system which can find *no* use for a man [like me] ... One could forgive the government for failing to employ the intelligentsia, who are on the whole politically unreliable ..."

I could quote many other sentiments of this sort, but every now and then his journalistic eye tells it as it is:

"14th September 1940: (London, The Blitz) On the first night of the barrage, which was the heaviest, they [anti-aircraft guns] are said to have fired 500,000 shells, i.e. at an average cost of £5 per shell, £2½ millions worth."

But the comment is back to form: "But well worth it, for the effect on morale".

But to finish on a quote, the most charitable to Orwell I could find:

"22nd April 1941: Have been two or three days at Wallington., Saturday night's blitz could easily be heard there – 45 miles distant. Sowed while at Wallington 40 or 50 lbs of potatoes, which might give 200 to 600 lbs according to the season, etc. It would be queer – I hope it won't be so, but it quite well may – if, when this autumn comes, those potatoes seem a more important achievement than all the articles, broadcasts, etc., I shall have done this year."

19th February 1994

By the time you read these words you will have surely seen the video, read the story in the newspapers and heard all about it through the grapevine.

The 'state' of Wanstonia is different in nature to all other states we, as anarchists, have consistently opposed. In the light of the nature of this particular emergent state is this something we can, or have to, come to terms with?

Many people regard the existence of Wanstonia as an incredible occurrence, and before 16th February with its tremendous impact, something in the nature of a fantasy.

However, Wandstonia has been *de facto* recognised by the fifth estate (by the main newspapers and the main television stations) so it is by no means a finished issue.

Whatever the outcome, the recognition, however belated, of the sovereignty of Wandstonia has brought this anarchist-inspired 'state' very much into the political foreground.

Politically, this has come at the worst time for the beleaguered Conservative 'government' in the midst of arms sales scandals currently under investigation.

It is openly said that the M11 roadway contract was given to the builders after a £100,000 donation to Conservative Party funds. No government in living memory has been hanging on, without an ounce of support in the country, for so long. But whether the government is now forced to resign is not so important to us as the consideration, which is no longer remote, of a complete change in political structures, of which this Wandstonian type of anarchist thinking is one of the examples.

We must not forget also that it was another extremely serious, effective, but brilliantly good-humoured anarchist group, the working Class War, which brought down the previous government, although it also enabled a *coup* to take place in true Banana Republic style, which secured the sneaky premiership of the present prime minister who is still hanging on to office. That the banana skin on which the Conservative adventurers should slip was to be seven well-designed houses with gardens for family occupation in Wanstead, was difficult to foresee.

From now on events will escalate at a rapid pace, the M11 Link Campaign has announced 'operation roadblock' starting 15th March.

The only reason that the Ministry of Transport was able to mount this operation was because a vast amount of money was spent on procuring labour. It was admitted by the 'government' side that costs of £200,000 were incurred *on the day alone* on payments to 800 police officers, 200 riot police, 700 reserves, plus the bailiffs and their mechanical equipment.

That anarchist economics *works* was actively demonstrated once again. The defenders were all sovereign individuals who contributed their own sovereigns and the anarchist side of the operation cost nothing. That is the simple fact of anarchist economics: nobody, not the 300 occupiers nor the 200 sympathisers, were there because of 'payment'. No money would have been adequate 'payment' for this resistance. As Aeschylus put it in his play for the Persians, *nun uper panton agon* (the fight is now for you all).

The confrontation was deadly. Everybody there hated the futility of it all, but the drama had to be enacted, *nobody was willing to stop this farce of communal ineptitude.*

Silver gave the commands which only Gold could countermand. No, this is not a line of a poem but the code-names which the police used on the day to disguise the names of their commanders.

Talking of videos, it would be good to know if anybody has compiled a list of films which document anarchist activities. The excellent *Dare to Dream* by Marianne Jenkins comes to mind. It would be good to refresh memories of glorious doings in the past. I personally was reminded of Wanstead's proximity to Ilford where there was a lot of squatting activity in the '60s with ample television coverage but without success. I remember a brilliant documentary by Monica Foot on a commercial channel which lingered on a *Freedom* headline: "Defend the Homeless!"

5th March 1994

It occurred to me, the day being the Ides of March, to glance at William Shakespeare's play of *Julius Caesar*. I could not get past the first lines and the significance they hold, which I previously missed:

Act one, Scene one: *the scene is Rome. A street. Enter the tribunes Flavius and Marullus, and certain commoners.*
Flavius: Hence! Home you idle creatures, get you home:
Is this a holiday? What! Know you not,
Being mechanical you ought not walk
Upon a labouring day without the sign
Of your profession? Speak, what trade art thou?
First commoner: Why, sir, a carpenter.
Marullus: Where is thy leather apron and thy rule?
... Wherefore are thou not in thy shop today?"

Clearly here is a description of communal life as Shakespeare imagined it to have taken place in Rome, but instantly recognisable as in his own time. The state was all powerful and the Romans pushed their noses into every aspect of life. How dare a mere carpenter show his face in public, the day not a holiday?

Unfortunately this brutal scene, meant to be funny and vulgar, does not continue in the same vein, even if seriously, to describe the arrangements and working conditions in Shakespeare's England or in Rome or wherever?

Restrictions on citizens remain, without a qualitative change.

Of all local authorities is the firm masquerading as London Transport the most vindictive? Posters are pasted up everywhere, with typography at its most obnoxious by a very reliable hand, with warning of instant fines on some poor travellers who cannot afford the fare.

Which reminds me of something a bit more constructive – visit to the Falls Road, Belfast (*Theatre Ireland*, no. 28, *Duchas na Saoirse* issue):

"Black taxis picked up passengers. This is an admirable idea born in Belfast, an impromptu community taxi service which went up and down the length of the Falls Road from the city centre to Andersonstown and back. The fare in 1989 was 35p and the first person in decided the direction. Other passengers waited at the kerb, hailing down the taxis. Thus the people have overcome a tardy bus service. Whether it was against the law or not, the people stamped their approval on the scheme and it worked."

S till on transport, it is my impression this sunny day that by and large the population has not appreciated the seriousness of the situation. To take one example: British Rail is truncated yet again, prior to selling off.

Nuclear waste is transported to Sellafield and back to the ports (Dover) by rail at the moment. In London it is carried on the North London Line. If the new owners pass these orders on to road transport, the trucks will use any routes available, neglecting communal safety conditions.

Nuclear waste trains and trucks on the motorways, red routes and country lanes will prove the most catastrophic enterprise that the executive have so far sanctioned.

A correspondent writes from Spain: "... regarding the obituary of Federica Montseny in *Freedom* (vol. 55, no. 3), there was some follow-up in the Spanish press – pieces, some much warmer, and an official commemoration in the national library, rather low key perhaps but the government is in a bit of trouble."

2nd April 1994

Languages blend into each other. The words 'anarchist' and 'organism' are both of Greek origin. The language in which these words are supposed to be written is modern English, although close scrutiny of the above words will find among them few if any 'English' words. If it were my task to translate even the gist of what is being said here purely in English without any adhesion of foreign words, I would have to throw up my hands in desperation (and no doubt never catch them in the descent) and throw in the towel altogether. Here we reach the nub or difficulty of the problem for those engaged in the diffusion of anarchist ideas among the natives of the British Isles whose *education* from *elementary school* to *university* has been foisted on them by *benevolent invaders* and *tyrants*. All the *italicised* words show the extent of *subjection* and *quod erat demonstrandum* need not be pursued here.

A word on why the concept of organisation is shortened to organism and why its usage is preferred. Anarchists are the only political animals (cf. Aristotle) who are interested in the organism (body) for its own sake and not for its abstract qualities. The word 'organ' from which both words derive is of Greek origin and merely means an instrument. Words are like chameleons or colours which change within the text or can only be defined by their surroundings (cf. colour theory). This again cannot be pursued here.

In a recent article for *Freedom* I quoted the exceptional Scots poet Robert Burns who is instantly understandable and who, to my knowledge, never used any word which was not *frae* and *fiere*.

You may notice how the sudden change from imported words sticks out like a sore thumb in the agglutinised mess which must remain the necessary style for the subject in hand.

The word 'anarchist' presents no less of a difficulty. It has to be translated and explained and its derivation copied out of uninformative history books which seem to agree that it is of Greek origin at around the time 404BC when in Athens there was a state of society without any government, the real meaning of it as far as my understanding of Greek is concerned, which might come as a surprise to all and sundry, is simply *lack of a leader*. In other words, we are talking about a natural order expressed as a political system.

It would have been far better had the anarchist revolution already succeeded, for then we would be already living in a *society* (from which the meaningless word 'socialism') which respects you and me and all our foibles and fancies and our very important material *and* abstract needs.

But we cannot change words to suit pragmatic needs. We hold on to the few attempts and the few people *who risked their life and their sanity*, who have been cut up into ribbons by those of all political persuasions who hold on to power for no other reason than for the sake of power, for the exhilaration, for the ride and for the glory, for the thrill of the moment of triumph over the vanquished.

Even in these islands, where are they now the early inhabitants still speaking their own language until they are pushed into the sea or live with the goats and sheep in inaccessible terrain. They pay the price for underestimating Caesar, whose navy of conquest initially floundered and yet were allowed to return and conquer and defeat what was an anarchist island, whose language is now lost in the mists of time, who committed all to memory and were defeated by the systematic scribes whose knowledge was in the written word, which is the ultimate power.

Anarchy versus despotism. What is the strength of your word if your signature, your seal, your minted coin is thrown in the trash can?

Say that you have known a thoroughly unworthy person (not the one you glimpse in the mirror but somebody who has proved to be the most asociable creature, say a politician who puts a whole town on the dole, or just a small entrepreneur who swindled the widow and the orphan) would you give such a person a letter of recommendation to a country and its people he/she may wish to visit? Certainly, upright citizen, you would do no such thing. But your country does. There is his passport duly stamped, all he has to prove is his birth of origin, another piece of paper.

What ancient inhabitant can resist that piece of paper which makes you homeless, which commits you to jail, which allows you so much pittance, which forbids you entrance, which closed down your factory, your hospital, which buries your rivers, asphalts your arable land.

And yet, like a canvas which once has been the work of a master but other hands have covered over layer by layer, a careful restorer might bring back to its original hues (O.E. sound), the cunning meaning of anarchy may be recovered not by the copyist, not by the party-man, but by those with the will and the wish to wash away the stains of tyranny.

How long is a piece of string? This is the question to which the answer cannot be learnt from books. Most anarchists know the answer to this riddle. It is the organism that matters, not the organisation, it is the return of respect for the umbilical cord. It is in tying and untying the knots which distinguish the anarchist from the impatient, clumsy tyrant cutting with his sword the Gordian knot which proved nothing but his ignorance.

Exiles have come to this land, perhaps they never knew why, and laboriously learnt the words of the language hoping that by knowing the words they could get to know the social arrangements. They could have saved their efforts in that direction, for nothing the natives liked more than putting their face sideways to the ground as with puckered mouths they blew at the kindling to light up their campfires.

16th April 1994

Writing a column for *Freedom* since January of this year has been a stimulating experience which I would like to share with you in brief. The first thing to remark on is the exceptional quality of the proof-reading by the editors. It is this care which distinguishes *Freedom*, and from this comes that feeling of overwhelming quality, despite, or because of, the poverty of its resources. Another gain has been that the assertion of my resolution not to read any other newspaper for a year as an experiment (*Freedom*, vol. 55, no. 1) except what is written in the anarchist press has been rewarded with insights into subjects I have always been interested in but had scarce time to consider.

Whatever the other papers hide in the sewers of Wapping, we have the best editorials, and what other paper has Colin Ward whose next instalment on wind power I awaited as eagerly as readers waited on the chapter of Charles Dickens – or was it Cervantes and the windmills?

Arthur Moyse is right to crow about the extra 25 pence on his old age pension; he always has known what's what. Once at the Golden Convulvulus trial (hands up who remember) Arthur introduced me as his nephew, which was fair enough – I always thought of him as my uncle.

Now that our defensive columnists are rushing to get protection from the official word-hoard, a quote from *Vanity Fair* will not go amiss. Becky Sharpe is leaving Miss Pinkerton's establishment:

"'Stop!' cried Miss Jemima rushing to the carriage with a parcel. '... Becky Sharpe, here's a book for you that my sister – that is I – Johnson's Dictionary, you know; you mustn't leave us without that. Goodbye. Drive on, coachman ...'

And the kind creature retreated into the garden, overcome with emotion.

But lo! and just as the coach drove off, Miss Sharp put her pale face out of the window, and actually flung the book back into the garden."

Reading nothing else but *Freedom* has certainly not improved my knowledge of meganews world politics. As a child I learnt the names of all countries and drew detailed maps of all continents. Today, many years later, I would need a refresher course. To keep up with the changes which daily take place would involve a very bright child's constant attention. Then there are the constant shufflings of the names in governments and in other executive organs which proliferate in this and every other nation state from Gaul to France and back. Is there a child out there being taught the names of the rulers east and west of the Urals?

The following item is also literature of the 'I've also been there' variety:

"The basement was dark, lit by candles and oil lamps. The young man was scarce fourteen. He was in a shelter and was sheltered by the refugees forced into the depths of the basements of their houses while the town shuddered under the mortar barrage and was carpet-bombed by metal albatrosses and in the night there were unusual sights to see for those young eyes in the basement's closeness and now in its farness. Humanity was good, humanity was kind, said the persecuted. A rather ailing woman gave him shelter. She began to think of him as if he were her own son. The parting, after the troubles ceased, was brutal. He returned to his family despite the woman's pathetic entreaties. 'Have I not been a good mother to you? Why leave me now when I love you so?' Nevertheless he went, but gave her a good length of cloth looted from the stores as a parting present. He never saw her again. His mother was overjoyed by his return, but chided him for squandering the length of cloth which, by rights, should have been hers."

30th April 1994

A narchist ideas have only half-heartedly entered the schooling-of-children system. I see the problem in the idea of the school itself. A school is a different place for the nursery child where it is sheer fantasy, a very potent enactment of communal dreaming. What is forgotten is that the very discontinuation of that schooling idea in the later stages causes the complete breakdown of society.

N ever before has the civil service been so humiliated than in the past fifteen years. Its role as the 'silent government' is now reduced to the status of subordinates who are paid to be told what to do.

A rt and anarchism sound harmoniously to my ears, whereas science and anarchism sounds restrictive. To offer an aphorism: science and art went up the hill to fetch a pail of water, science fell down and art came tumbling after.

R eturning to the subject of Anarchy in the UK, I see from the leaflet that the massive anarchist poetry anthology is on its way.

C irculation is a funny word, of blood, money and newspapers. Certainly all contributors would like to see *Freedom* being better circulated, especially by the momentous days of October when there will be a great upsurge of interest.

H ow many roads must a man walk down before you can call him a man? The person who asked this question was good at asking questions. He was particularly interested in white doves and cannon balls, but his choicest question was as to how long a mountain may exist before it's washed to the sea.

Y et another boat race come and gone. The Spartans have defeated Athens. The Cambridge crew uses Herculean methods of preparation, strenuous exercises including weight-lifting every morning of two tonnes of metal to increase their brain muscles. *Et in Arcadia Ego!*

14th May 1994

Mother knows best. No other person amongst us, except through imagination, experiences all that which adds up to living out a full life. I once saw a copy of *Mujeres Libres* (Free Women) which was published during the Spanish Revolution, and one glance showed the strength of the anarchist movement.

Until the human being learns to be unafraid of anything, most of all the self, it will be unable to co-operate. Without co-operation with others, all social groupings live in the shadow of fear.

The most we can hope for is that we can be understood by others with different understandings. Utopia is a romance by Thomas More of a perfect island. The word itself, ou topos from the Greek, contradictorily means no place, nowhere, hence Butler's *Erewhon*, William Morris's *News from Nowhere*. Carlyle's rendering it into the German 'Weissnichtwo' (don't know where) is charming and a little more hopeful.

A little knowledge is a dangerous thing. Yesterday I saw a creature so tiny yet so exuberantly vital (perhaps an inch long by two-sixteenths in diameter) floating in the air under a tree, its body twisting with the agility of a swimmer. So frail, so powerful. Flies have wings, they use power – this creature was just light enough for the air currents to cushion it and was wafted in all directions it wished to go. But thereby hangs the tail of my ignorance, for what I was observing was the common caterpillar hanging by the thread of its own creation. Not quite, but the nearest thing I have seen to freedom in action.

Law is an ass, but in the rulers' terms it is defined as the command of a sovereign, backed up by sanctions, and maintained by a habit of obedience. It also relies on the myth of the Original Contract.

All public life goes into reverse at the time of elections. That is the time when the public is toasted and buttered. This is when promises lull the electorate, while repression insinuates its ever-changing form.

Identity cards for the poor. Who knows whether the executive through its dictates, which need not go through Parliament, have already arranged to issue them through the 'benefits' system. This is a serious matter for the mass of the people. Poverty limits and confines people to stay in specified locations, a kind of open prison, with a recurring specified time for the roll-call.

Doubt not, however, the strength of the anarchist saying that 'Injustice to one is injury to all'. Or, to quote an old voice, 'What stronger breastplate than a heart untainted / Thrice is he arm'd that hath his quarrel just, / And he but naked, though lock'd up in steel, / Whose conscience with injustice is corrupted.'

28th May 1994

Grief is a comparatively new word – even if it sounds English like grave, gravitas and the rest, it conceals its ruling class Latin origin – whereas sorrow is as old as tears, grief has its political uses. The nation mourns its greatest son (nobody gave him a second thought while he was alive). Another nation (a republic no less) mourns the demise of its first lady queen (nobody remembers a single thing about her). The ex-prime minister (well, almost) contemplates living in a cardboard box on the Strand and grieves at the unsightly prospect. The future contender with the unfortunate name of Blair remembers a once-ambitious novelist who rejected the same and chose Orwell as his pen-name. Bad name for a politician and a godsend to lampoonists (remember the brilliant Rooum cartoon?) the shepherd and his flock, the faithful sheep blairing obediently.

Uppermost in everybody's mind is the coming festival season. Festival guides have replaced passports in their importance – and quite rightly, for knowing where the thing is at is more important than how to get in. There is always a gap in the fence. But because of the unwelcome attention of thugs (i.e. agents of government) what was openly advertised in the past is now given by word of mouth and at the shortest of notice. It is estimated that over a million people attended these festivals last year – a population on the move. There are now gatherings all over the country and these camps have really caught on in Russia, Spain and Slovenia. Those were the days, though, when there was an anarchist camp in Cornwall. Even if ideological differences between the French and Manchester comrades over the siting of lavatories have lost us the local farmers' goodwill. We had the best chef reduced to tears by the introduction of the rota system as he stood by waiting for his turn to stir the pot.

Note that the arming of the police in London was mooted by the tourist board to "reassure continental visitors". The taking of a million pounds for one year residences is part of a deal with the mafia.

L otteries are about as interesting as religion for vacant minds, and if the Italian method is going to be copied the numbers will be picked out of a revolving drum by young people specially chosen for their angelic looks. That the recipients of this windfall will come off a list of trusted government toadies is saying nothing new, for the winners of the premium bonds of the 'you've never had it so good' society are evenly distributed among the favoured sons of SAS, MI5 and the rest.

A nother joke is, in the worst possible taste, the Bill now nodded through the sleeping Commons nicknamed the 'Injustice Bill'. This is about the worst piece of legal rubbish that has ever been perpetrated and will be given the same treatment by the enraged populace as the poll tax. One thing it shows is that the executive have run out of legal prose stylists, unable to cope with the imprecision Major Major delights in. That this last piece of legislation by a discredited bunch of crooks will never be put into effect is little consolation for those who will be subjected to random violence given the rubber-stamp of the law. How anybody can define music (prosecutable) as a succession of "repetitive beats" is beyond comprehension. Another bit of the Bill is the most ridiculous thing since Lex invented the law. That is what is called the ex parte injunction (i.e. to make accusations about you without you being present or informed) and turf you out of your home within 24-hours on a bad-wishers' say-so, rubber-stamped by some hireling judge after payment of the appropriate fee. You cannot legislate against homelessness, but this Bill actively encourages private violence to be used by people who do not even have the remotest interest in the property involved. And how can you legislate against repetitive beats? And how can you legislate against three village philosophers walking along the road? All I can say is the sooner we shall have anarchy the better.

W hoever wrote the following is a far better writer than anybody the executive can produce on their pea processors:

"Anarchism is a definite intellectual current of social thought whose adherents advocate the abolition of economic monopolies and of all political and coercive institutions within society. In place of the capitalist economic order, anarchists would have a free association of all productive forces based upon cooperative labour, which would have for its sole purpose the satisfying of necessary requirements of every member of society."

Legislate against that, Major Major!

11th June 1994

Got our work cut out, haven't we comrades? From 'water for sale' to prezervation of ze English language to test tube babies (not in its old meaning). No doubt anarchists out there have already considered the implications of out-of body fertilisation, the joke is that thereby the human being is made redundant within foreseeable generations.

Energy is what all life-forms produce, by themselves and in co-operation with others from the simplest to the grandest. The trouble with Newsteinian postulates of matter being inanimate is that it is a clever way round to produce working equations, but missing the main point of all, that all energy systems are 'alive' and there is no point in quibbling about which is doing what. As they used to say in the scientific circles I used to move around in, we are all in the same soup.

Numbers are instructive. When two-thirds of the population have better things to do than putting idle crosses on ballot papers, it means people are beginning to see through the charade of politics.

Elections come and go, but the government will hang on until the last trickle of North Sea oil. Another sure sign of a debased currency is the size, frequency and quality of postage stamps.

Theatre, in all its aspects, was taught to me to no avail, for the theatre never employed me. Three plays of mine received three different treatments. My first was produced by my young friends and was interesting to do. The second was never produced, even a copy is no longer in existence. The third had two excellent readings and stopped there and then some five years ago. People are still interested but are deterred because it needs a cast of thousands. Most fringe theatres cannot cope with more than four actors who double the parts.

Interesting to read through anarchist papers left in old drawers. *Wildcat*'s editorial front page of its number one issue twenty years ago (1974) could be reprinted today without altering one word. The bit that starts: *"The British Army's occupation of Northern Ireland is a failure. It always was. The decision – by a Labour government – to send the troops in was an admission of failure in the first place ... For a fraction of what it costs British taxpayers to keep the soldiers where they are – miserable, hated and getting killed – the original demands for houses, jobs, an end to electoral gerrymandering, could have been met. But governments will always seek to save face rather than save people ... The alternative is more killing."*

Capitalism is playing havoc with the simplest and most trusted services. That hospitals now exist to make money out of patients and not to cure them is well known and there are tales too horrendous to mention. But what about the postal service? Once the post office is completely privatised, letters will have to be collected from the sorting offices. Perhaps we will have to telephone and ask 'any letters for me today?' The electronic answer will be swift: 'letters for you are awaiting collection at the sorting offices of Edinburgh, Newcastle, Fooey and Lisbon'. Just saddle up your horse and off you go. Far-fetched? An acquaintance in India waiting for his post was finally persuaded to break into the district office and liberate the mail addressed to him and his friends!

Since I've stopped reading other than anarchist newspapers I rely entirely on *Freedom*'s international coverage. The problem of translations (and they are excellent) is not only the language but the political slang that goes with it. The larger the anarchist movement the simpler the language becomes. We tend to understate things. News from abroad shows a great renewal of activity, but do comrades abroad know of the significance of the proposed October events in this locality? It must be important if the London Anarchist Forum cancels an evening in its stead. But as for the international news, can we have more of what is referred to as the 'Anarchist UPRISING in Mexico' which was evidently planned for ten years, but less of the other communiques which sound as if they emanate from Radio Albania at its most glutinous eras, as if they were written by comrades whose teeth were broken by their erstwhile masters.

25th June 1994

Perhaps the decision that I should not read other than the anarchist press will one day be appreciated by the world of music, for I have finally taught myself to play the guitar *and* the piano in the extra time provided and since then I have played on these unsuspecting instruments some interesting tunes and am able to report now that I can finally play to my own satisfaction a delightful food song by the composer Carey Blyton. The words by J.A. Lindon say all I can say, and better, about the present political situation: "Scouring out the porridge pot, / Round and round and round! / Out with the scraith and scroopery, / Lift the eely ooly droopery, Chase the glubbery slubbery gloopery / Round and round and round."

Anarchy in the UK (the October event) is proceeding apace. It is something to look forward to. What interest me most is what I shall think of it in November after all those hundreds of events which have taken place. It will show in no uncertain manner the amount of support forthcoming from the population at large. The anarchist movement has always been good at protest, now could be the time for all and everyone to see and experience the harmonious nature of living in an anarchist society.

The late prevalence of a close and confined atmosphere has been rather favourable to the growths of weeds, observed Sam Weller. Now that I have little time to attend to such matters, I have been wondering why have weeds received such bad press. What others regard as weeds would feed the whole population.

Information is a thorny process. Much of the knowledge of today will have been forgotten by tomorrow. What interests me might not interest others. To live an open life is an anarchist characteristic. We are what we are. There are long security files on people who live today. Hundreds of years ago similar files existed on other people. A famous author, Thomas Kydd – what remains of him? Not one letter, not one signature, not one book has been attributed to him with certainty, yet he shared a bench with Christopher Marlowe and his *The Spanish Tragedy* is an outstanding masterpiece. Yet there was surveillance on him every adult day of his life. He was supposed to have written the *Ur-Hamlet*, but no copy exists.

Elbow grease is the best furniture oil, but however hard you polish the old table it does not take long for somebody else to scratch his name in it.

Not quite sure if it was the same Guy Fawkes who said: "Desperate diseases require desperate remedies".

Cuddling may well become the subject of the latest Home Office inquiry and may well be considered to be made illegal. Highly-paid experts at the Home Office have discovered that cuddling leads to anti-social and deviant behaviour.

Eras come and go. It used to be a craze to try to give the exact date of historical events. The most amusing is the era of Abraham which was given as 1st October 2016bc. The least amusing is the one that began 6th August 1945.

9th July 1994

Remarkable, and who would have thought that quicksilver has been used for centuries by dentists in amalgams to stop teeth without any reported side effects. The material was considered inert, now there are doubts and fears that fumes of mercury enter vital organs of the body. The safest filling is with copper or gold – unfortunately a price tag is attached to these metals under capitalism. It is puzzling how many materials are considered safe for human use until evidence to the contrary becomes overwhelmingly obvious. Only fifty years ago asbestos was considered in all aspects an excellent insulator, until it was found that filaments entering through breathing destroyed the lungs.

You may have seen old mirrors, which sparkle with mercury coating. This method of silvering looking-glasses went on for ages in spite of the pernicious effects of mercury upon the tradesmen. Mercury is regarded as a metal although it is fluid at ordinary temperatures. It is also typical of the haphazardness of scientific nomenclature that the planet Mercury has no quicksilver but is named after fleet-footed Hermes.

Perhaps there is a slow progress in medicine after all, for liquid mercury is no longer used, although at the beginning of this century it was occasionally given with the view of overcoming, by weight, obstructions in the intestinal canal.

Each day brings its wonders. Outside the Nigerian Embassy, opposite their dusty windows with their curious contents without the slightest hint of past glories of the Benin culture, someone placed a chair. On it was a ghetto-blaster and a handwritten placard with the wording: 'IT IS HIGH TIME TO STOP THE BULLY-BOY TACTICS'! While I was pondering over the meaning of this delphic utterance, an affable young man arrived and said without further ado: "People say I'm foolish. What I say is that everything has to have a beginning, however small."

State is an historically temporary arrangement, a transitory form of society, in the dismissive words of Michael Bakunin.

I joined a walk on its second day from Farnborough to London protesting against the sale of Hawk military aircraft to the temporary arrangement, the Indonesian state, which uses Hawks to suppress the East Timor people, by another temporary arrangement calling itself British Aerospace. It was a pleasant walk with my companions on a sunny day from Chertsey to Kingston through country lanes and by the Thames river bank. Here were less than a dozen people, distributing leaflets as they went. All beginnings are small. I specifically like the acronym (I would, wouldn't I) for this group: ARROW (Active Resistance to the Roots of War).

S*omer is icumen in. Lhude sing cuccu.* As long as they are not repetitive beats, for under the new law the bird will be liable to arrest, and the number of prosecutions against the ringers and tollers of church bells will increase a thousandfold.

There is no accounting for taste. It is difficult to decide which is my current favourite poem. The one which I recently came across is by Edwin Morgan and has the title 'The Loch Ness Monster Song'. I tried to sing it without success, but it remains a test for typesetting. I don't know if it is as beautiful as the earliest known English round quoted above. This one is a bit more difficult to read but contains the immortal question and answer: *'Hovoplodok – dovoplodock – plovodokot – dpolokodosh?' 'Splgraw fok fok splgrafhatchgabrigabrl fok slfok!'*

23rd July 1994

These words are written in the evening after the demonstration (24th July) against the proposed Criminal *In*justice Bill. The demonstration was organised by an ad hoc group 'Building the Coalition'. Although advance publicity was minimal, the crowd that gathered filled Trafalgar Square and its surrounds. The march started from Hyde Park to hear the speakers, including trade unionists who denounced the Labour Party's stand on this issue.

By and large it was a joyous gathering, confident and assertive – in this respect the coalition worked very well. But the acceptance of the route of the march dictated by Traffic Control caused a few problems. The route went through the least populous, on a Sunday, but most dangerous part of London which took in heavily defended government and business interests. This gave a chance for the authorities to show off new and old weaponry and produced at least one irrelevant confrontation near Mr Major's residence where the tall gates, and dogs and their handlers behind them, defended the bastion such as it is. As news information is controlled by the government the slightest error will be magnified and the population at large will give credence to the propaganda.

An anarchist-organised demonstration would not have allowed a public control enforced route away from the populations of Oxford and Regent Streets, Piccadilly Circus, Charing Cross Road – a scenic route urbanely more invigorating than the deadly meandering around parks Hyde and Green, encountering strongly defended points, with only one upstairs window on the whole route without a surveillance camera. The state's champions – armed gangsters in film-set costumes – defended whatever they were ordered to defend, from a hamburger eatery to the revamped Westminster Abbey and Big Ben showing different times on their po-faced clocks. Reaching Downing Street all it took was for one superb young athlete to climb the iron gate in great Olympic style for the officer in command to give his long-awaited opportunity for action. The dog-handlers let loose their dogs to savage the young man. As the crowd on the other side of the gate shouted in impotent rage, the officer sent in the *police horses* to clear innocent bystanders.

No doubt this publicity stunt by this officer made sure that the know-alls of the readers of the mass circulation papers will all tell you 'Oh yes, the demonstration in Trafalgar Square ... the police had to bring in their horses'.

A similar event occurred at Glastonbury. Over a quarter of a million people living for a few days in peace and harmony, authority safely locked out, to be told three days later 'Must have been terrible with all that violence'.

As to any formal anarchist presence, I did not see any copies of *Freedom* for sale. There was a copy of *Anarchy UK* handed to me and also a well-written article/leaflet from the ACF, who also manned a useful information stall in the square.

To end on a cheerful note, I was glad to see a cycling combine of four riders who, by their own exertions, pedalled enough power to produce amplified music and in the square provided the only amplification for the speakers.

But that the movement is young, confident and boisterously assertive of its rights, there should be no doubt. That the government gets the service it pays for, and no more, is also obvious.

6th August 1994

Lo and behold, one of the few advertisements in the Underground system which was vetoed to be shown to the GP (as the General Public is laughingly referred to) was a poster designed and paid for by the Levellers music ensemble. I wonder what dreadful revelations were contained in the advertisement that our ever-loving executive objected to people seeing. Can it be possible that it had something to do with the recent Trafalgar Square gathering (to protest against the Criminal Justice Bill) and the imminent release of the new anarchist golden oldie 'Why so Unhappy, Old Blue and True?' and on the flip-side 'Happy days are Here Again'?

Every minute a cargo of cooped-up humans passed through the air space above the garden of the house not as much as a quarter of a mile atop our distinguished heads. Imagine the roar these machines produce and that is life beneath the flight path to London's airport. The number of people passing over that garden in their pressurised cabins is estimated to add up in a year of traffic to a colossal number of something like 916 (wait for it) million people. It is that roar we hear.

Vacation time at Westminster. Would anybody notice if the members never returned? But they'll be back to pick up their cheques and to sign on the dotted line.

Electronic mail has broken through the barriers of privilege. The French revolution was greatly assisted by the preparatory work of the encyclopaedists who "were tainted by impracticable revolutionary ideas".

Limited choice is all we have, although some people maintain choice is endless. Perhaps the only choice we have is Hobson's choice. Hobson kept horses for hire and he gave you the choice of hiring any of them as long as you took the horse which stood already harnessed "nearest the stable door".

Life in an anarchist society should be made less difficult than it is now. Consider mother. She is willing to carry a child into the world and allows her body to take her through all the loops the body is capable. It does not stop there. Before a child is weaned it must also be understood. As the months and years go by, the intellectual contact must be made. Something is gained: a new entity. Something is lost and must be found: equilibrium.

Education is an art of drawing out the faculties. From an old manual: "*The business of education involves two main considerations: 1. What to teach? and 2. How to teach it?*" But typically no answers are given.

Radioactive nuclear waste is carried by train (not usually at weekends) through North London. Last Saturday all traffic was diverted from the Chalk Farm area. Conflicting reasons were given, such as an accident with an oil lorry. The people working in the nearby market said a train was involved.

Speakers' Corner is reduced in size once more. The builders are in and they have sliced a good third off it. So another restriction on the 'valve of free speech' where people used to let off steam.

Those who know PS (Philip Sansom) would have been delighted to hear his name mentioned so admiringly on Radio 4 last week. On a programme called 'The Soap Box' Joan Lestor said how privileged she was to have heard him at Speakers' Corner speaking for the anarchists. Where are the new orators today?

20th August 1994

We like drawing imaginary lines and although the sky through the large windows looks the same to me whichever way I look, when I go through that door marked 'Embarkation' I am shepherded to another country. It is a bit like going to the cinema. You buy your ticket at the box office and you can go through the door and watch the film.

Leaving the country is usually easy. They are only too pleased to see the back of you. Returning is a different story altogether.

Mind you, there are formalities, such as passports and money. It's a bit like a Turkish bath – from ice cold water to the steaming hot.

And all that geography! The sun shining on that placid wave is where England ends and France or Spain begins.

Whatever, it is a huge industry. You may recall my calculations (there must be a maths master out there who could check it for me) that within twelve months 916 million people go through the air space of any ordinary garden on the flightpath to London airport. That journey also started the same way. All they had to do was to go through a door flourishing tickets, passports and money. Once they are in the aircraft – where are they? Over our heads making a lot of noise.

Money is good for business. especially taking money off travellers on ships, at embarkation points or in the city centres. The money-changer is on to a good thing. He buys cheap and sells dear – and makes a fixed charge for his work plus commission.

The coach arrived in Plymouth at 5am and it was raining heavily. But the old man and his wife were opening the café, an enormous barn of a place.

"You run this place on your own?" I asked incredulously.

"My son helps, but he doesn't get up early." He was eager to explain his circumstances and suddenly my eyes filled with tears. Maybe I was tired from the journey, but that is a simplification.

The old man was a Greek Cypriot from the village of Muffli in Turkish-occupied Cyprus (imaginary lives and their consequences once again).

"We were told to leave our homes in two hours – we lost all our belongings. My wife wasn't even allowed to take a change of clothing."

His wife was standing behind the counter squirting hot water into the teapot and gently put finger across her mouth signalling him to be quiet. "The gentleman doesn't want to know" she said.

This is when suddenly tears were pouring out of my eyes.

I recalled another story told to me recently by a Turkish Cypriot woman. It was the 'other side' which messed up her life and her family's. "They treated me like a piece of luggage from the age of two. I've never got over it."

Victoria station was deserted on Tuesday evening. 'The pain of it all' said a poster put out by the management. A few people were sitting about. The polished floors would make an excellent ballroom.

The problem about railways is that, unlike shipping, it is almost like a Rubic's cube exercise of rushing empty trains across long distances to be in readiness for the following morning's passenger transport. There was no point in having the trains in Victoria, where they stood empty at night on 27 platforms and dozens of sidings, when all that stock was needed in commuter country in the morning to bring the 'workers' into the city.

Come an anarchist society the rail track could easily be converted for the use of roller-skaters and skate-boarders.

17th September 1994

Perhaps there is no such thing as insular politics and my experiment of not reading the 'national papers' is proving to be correct. Here in Madrid, even with my rudimentary knowledge of the lingo it is obvious that all that percolates from the UK is a tired story about royalty and 'profiles' of entertainers. Even Burgess, a very knowledgeable writer, didn't believe in the existence of England and thought that London was the capital of Ireland. In *El Mundo*, the daily newspaper, the only reference I could find to the existence of our beloved country is one line giving the exchange rate of the 'libra enteplice' at 199.808 pesetas.

What is agitating the newspapers here is the equivalent of what agitates our papers at home – the extradition of peoples from Uruguay and France, forest fires, illegal immigrants arriving in ramshackle vessels south of Spain and, of course, the saga of Cubans sailing to Florida.

What is more heartening from an anarchist point of view is that I could purchase a monthly *CNT* newspaper from the local kiosk in a very undistinguished part of Madrid, and I also encountered an anarchist bookstall at the local flea market at the Tirso de Molina, which can be found there every Sunday. The red and black flag is also flying proudly over the large and busy offices of the CNT.

The main articles – which I found very well argued and easy to read, having been brought up on *Freedom* editorials – concerned the role of the G7, its bid for world domination and the role of the international 'peace-keeping' force. Another article, by Paco Cabello, analysed the nature of the yearly occurrence of forest fires, the resultant loss of land and governmental incompetence and lack of concern, in a very similar way to what is happening in the UK.

Except for centres (towns, cities) Spain is a barren land and under-populated. The jargon of capitalism is probably most confident here than at home, and the musical and motor-engine phrase 'fine tuning' is the easy expression used by triumphant economists as the industries sack thousands of workers, ensuring high profits for the few.

But, in conversations with comrades here, the anarchist movement in Spain can do no more than to consolidate its position for the time being. The reputation of the CNT here is very high and its straight-forward solidarity with the workers in all circumstances gives it (I can't find another word) an 'affectionate' look. Can you imagine a local union at home being treated as implicitly.

As for prices here, they are about the same as in the UK. Politicians at Westminster may froth about the white heat of technology, but there seems to be an irreversible downward slide at home compared to things here.

Slogans and wild gestures are of little use. Unless we can create an organisation which is both known and respected and can achieve some cohesiveness, the future, from this distance, looks bleak.

1st October 1994

At the recent anti Criminal Justice Bill demonstration, Jeremy
Corbyn MP gave prior notice of plans by the 'Michael Howard
Home Office plc' to issue national identity cards. This is the usual
insane effort on the part of the authorities to pretend that there is such
a thing as complete and successful surveillance. The mania for
identity cards is just a money-making ploy. The photographs and the
plastic have to be paid for. However automated an office might be,
the staff has to be increased to deal with 55 million bits of separate
individuals. Updating them with their secret code information is a
tragic joke comparable to the work of Hercules cleaning up the
Aegean stables, except a little bit more smelly and difficult. Perhaps
they would also like an instant census, all present and correct, sir,
press a button and the whole population will jump to attention.

At the same demonstration – which was still peaceful despite great
provocation until I left it – going home unfortunately we were not
allowed to go down Oxford Street (the tube at Marble Arch was closed
and we wanted to walk to Bond Street, the nearest station). We were
met by a cordon of police who refused us entry into Oxford Street.
Conversation with an unwilling member:
Q: Why can't we walk down Oxford Street?
A: Don't know. You can't.
Q: Who can tell me?
A: Ask the commanding officer.
Q: Where is he?
A: Don't know. Now move along.
So how could there have been a riot in Oxford Street when it was
closed end to end, cordoned off by police? Was the cordon abandoned
to allow a contingent specially hired for the occasion, with the
co-operation of the *Times* and the *London Evening Standard*, to break
at least one shop window and by doing so divert the attention of the
next day's newspapers from the brutal crowd management tactics and
risible incompetence of the Home Office plc?

I saw with my own eyes how the police in combat uniforms, together
with a squadron on horseback, were constantly menacing the young
people around the corner of Park Lane and Speakers' Corner. What
was their crime? They were joyous, and I for one liked their very
cheerful music, very clever with simple good lyrics, and I go along
with and admire their simple assertion of their human rights – their
right 'to party' and they *were* having a party under intolerable
conditions, their sound systems being pushed back inch by inch from
Park Lane to Speakers' Corner, physically pushed back in their

peaceful thousands by frustrated gents wearing ridiculous uniforms with the proto-design identity cards pinned to their ample chests.

Whoever organised the mayhem it wasn't the anarchists, but the same kind of bungler – the difference is only qualitative – the same executive decision as when the US hierarchy ordered the dropping of a nuclear bomb on its own people. Here was a right ying-yang for everybody, as they used to say in the '60s.

This is a phlegmatic, polite and even docile country, and yet were there not marksmen standing on tops of houses, was there not a huge intruding noisy motorised zeppelin flying over our heads advertising a lemon or some such citrus fruit and cunningly filming and photographing every member of that huge crowd, same as three days later in sunny charming Bournemouth where an unprecedentedly large procession besieged the Tory Party conference making the Tory rent-a-crowd shake with indignation. Disgraceful, they shouted, how dare these people protest against the curtailment of their civil liberties. On the television set it was left to a police superintendent (he will soon get the sack) to have to defend his decision even *to allow* such a demonstration to take place.

Interviewer: Don't you think it was reckless on your part to allow this demonstration to take place [turning aside and reading from a prepared script] in view of the riots [*sic*] last Sunday in Hyde Park.

Superintendent: [grinning] These people had proper permission. I would have looked foolish to ban a demonstration which was protesting in a peaceful manner against the curtailment of their right to protest.

Cut to a clip of a young Tory (mentally not a day older than 85) who was given time to whimper "These people are not representative. Look at them, they are scum, [spluttering] these people are the corrupters of the public *morale*" (he meant morality – a revealing Freudian slip).

So while the Tories were practising their oratory inside the ugly looking Business Centre, the procession wound along the leafy lanes, good humoured and peaceful (except for a bit of mechanical shouting of a sloppy slogan the SWP equates with revolution). The home-made placards were much more to the point, such as 'Hands Off My DNA', 'Gerroff Moi Rights', even a pun on the latest Tory Party slogan 'Britain is Getting Stranger'. You won't read this anywhere else except in *Freedom*, but I did see the population lining the streets and cheering.

But for the zeppelin above our heads making an awful racket, the sign of a government having lost the support of the population and falling back on technological defence, the aim of the organisers, who all live in Bournemouth, coupling their implacable opposition to the *In*justice Bill with the physical fact of the Tory Party jamboree in Bournemouth itself, have been fully justified.

May you live in interesting times, goes the old Oriental saying. My favourite slogan at the moment is 'Demons Out'. Who would have thought that metaphysics would ever have a new relevance. Cool heads and warm hearts, comrades, there is a lot of work to do.

29th October 1994

My belated visit to Spain has put a lot of things into focus which I should have understood better at about the time of the 1960s when I was an editor of *Freedom*. It seems to me now that there is nothing like a first-hand experience. All editors of *Freedom* should take a sabbatical every now and then and visit Spain and see for themselves. Of course, one can come away with some strange ideas after only one short visit.

Spain is the home of anarchism and as such has provided a model for the rest of the world. Anarchist politics in this country in the '60s, when our movement began to grow, always held up the Spanish anarchist ideal. Today the need for an anarchist movement has never been stronger and we can still learn a lot from our Spanish comrades. There is still a huge following of anarchism in Spain. Every district, from the smallest to the largest towns, has an anarchist group. It is without question that the dictates of its geography have quite a lot to do with it, the varying climate of Spain practically spells out the need for autonomous communities. Each district has a very strong social cohesion, necessarily different in the harsh climate of the Asturias to the torpid heat of Andalucia. Whatever the government tried to do, it can't stop the siesta. The weather dictates the behaviour pattern of the population. When the sun is at its zenith, the population of the south re-assert themselves and shut the door on the crazy outside world. At night they sit out under the canopy of stars and settle all scores in a kind of unofficial parliament, open and unashamed.

If comrades want anarchism here they should consider, as good Kropotkinians all, the weather. We can always get rid of this government, or any government, but we cannot change the climate. This being anarchist poetry year, the following lines by Louis MacNeice will reinforce the sentiment:

"The glass is falling hour by hour, / The glass will fall forever, / But if you break the bloody glass / You won't hold up the weather."

So the government (the corrupt body of men and women dedicated to killing off, poisoning and otherwise disposing of by wars, pestilence and any other means at hand, the entire population including their own granny if need be) has published another binding law, which Major's favourite author Lombroso had written out painstakingly only a hundred years ago: how to criminalise the entire population. Here we have the corporate state, timidly respectful trade unions, unctuous press and pulpit, a nicely combed opposition and the voice of Edwina Curry is heard all over the land.

It has to be said by somebody, though, that the anarchist movement will not be intimidated. The authorities have tried before and they have failed. They can pass as many stupid laws as they wish. Anarchism had a mass following in Spain. It is no longer a minority movement here. An injury to one is an injury to all. We must give clear warning that the anarchist movement will not tolerate the harassment of a single individual by the state. Everyone who is victimised for one reason or another should know that there is an anarchist group nearby who will do their utmost to avert private or communal catastrophe.

As for Anarchy in the UK – following the ten days of festivities the response from all concerned was very positive and it looks like we are going to have an even bigger and better one in 1995.

12th November 1994

L ondon has borne the brunt of this country's political activities for too long. Compared to other capital cities, it is a difficult place to live in, especially as there is a lack of municipal acumen which such a metropolis demands by its very nature. Visiting other cities in the country there are only a few which are beset by similar difficulties, such as the seats of government (Westminster), seats of finance (City of London) and a focal point for tourism.

Scotland's capital cities perhaps are beset only by the latter consideration. Nobody knows if Cornwall or Wales have any capital cities. As for Ireland, Stormont in Belfast has been abolished, which leaves only one civic power in Ireland – that which resides in Dublin.

However controversial the above may be, from an anarchist point of view and from the point of view of somebody who either lives or works in London, the anarchist movement has seen more political activity in London than in other parts of the country.

Should government move out of Westminster or the City of London go bankrupt, both a very likely event only a few years ago but now as real power has shifted politically to Brussels and financially to Tokyo, London can easily become a ghost town in which, like in many other towns in these isles, a third of the population is without a job and lives on hand-outs.

The above remarks (cryptic admittedly, but surely understandable to readers who in 1962 were deemed by a devoted questioner to "be highly intelligent") are after all addressed to the incipient anarchist movements on these isles.

The reference to Dublin, which cannot have but one tenth of the problems of London, is that it is nevertheless a civic power, same as Westminster, with a military pocket in Ulster/Northern Ireland which is under military rule.

The present talks are a farce and everybody should know it. The troops should be withdrawn forthwith. As for London, the same for Belfast. There is now talk of restarting the Anarchist Federation of Britain, but first of all local federations need to be put in place. Such as the Administration of Anarchist Activities of London, Isle of Man, Cambridge, Belfast, etc. The title AFB is a misnomer and only vaguely points at a direction. But it is significant that even the highly successful Anarchy in the UK '94 had to take place in London. Next year allow a Londoner to suggest that Anarchy in the UK should take place simultaneously in all the suffering capital towns – Glasgow, London, Belfast or even Dublin. Surely anarchists do not believe in frontiers?

Visiting my local community centre I carefully looked at the noticeboard, the contents of which could easily fill, and no doubt interest, readers of this paper. Every time I visit the Freedom Bookshop their wall for similar and different notices is completely full. The person who runs this noticeboard at the community centre takes, I am told, at least an hour a day putting up the notices and carefully filing the old ones. There must be hundreds of these noticeboards now in London and they serve a very useful service. Just to give an idea to readers of the range of interests appealed to on this randomly selected noticeboard, I venture to give the whole list. I wonder if people realise how much love and attention to detail characterises these cheaply put out communications. This is the whole list as I copied it out from left to right:

Global Partnership (conference) / Visions of Poesy (book jacket) / Survivors of the Mental Health System / Music concert (benefit) / Poetry readings schedule / Book list / Storytelling ceilidh / Photographic Society (leaflet) / Tree dressing event / Bicycle maintenance workshop / Anti-Criminal Justice Bill week of activities / Stop the CIA week / Benefit for Mordecai Vanunu / Stop the Hawks / Flysheet Camp (holidays for urban children in the countryside) / Women's art group / Age Concern / Art therapy / M11 Campaign / Lancashire hot spots / Piano tutor / Free Information Network (contacts list with 256 addresses) / Technology course / Local history studies / River Action / Recycling / Tenants Federation news / Anti-whaling leaflet.

No doubt there are noticeboards all over the town in colleges and offices. However you usually need a rubber stamp from the principal's office before the leaflet is displayed.

I find such noticeboards full of information and I wonder how they will get comprehensive attention.

A correspondent asked, in jest of course, that if I were so clever could I inform the writer of the exact time of the coming anarchist revolution. As this is not the first time that I and many other comrades have been asked precisely the same question, I've decided to make some culminations (oops, calculations). After a pleasurable hour or so with pencil and paper, I can now give the exact time for such an event to take place at 5.00pm on 16th November 1999. If anybody wishes to verify this all they need is a pencil and paper and a few pleasurable hours to spare.

26th November 1994

Popular preconceptions still abound on the nature of the universe. That 50% of thinking (?) people in the US still believe that the Sun revolves around the Earth shows the strength of their educational system in its inverse proportions. I've mentioned before the bewildering fact that some of the knowledge of ancient times practically disappears for a thousand years and I quoted the case of the Latin author Tacitus whose work was suppressed by the church for many centuries. I have recently come across the work of the African author Matianus Capella whose work, written in the fifth century AD, only surfaced a thousand years later (to be derided), nevertheless in his chapter on astronomy in which Venus and Mercury are described to go round the sun, a book known to Copernicus, he had important things to say.

How such suppression takes place can easily be explained by present-day examples. Many works of art suffer such a fate. It is good to hear that there is an exhibition of 'Unshowables', works of art which disappeared into the vaults of public collections never to see daylight again. Richard Niman's polychrome sculpture was bought by the Imperial War Museum (the sculpture shows a marked similarity to a well-known mid-century eccentric who is shown tearing a baby doll to bits) and never exhibited.

In the beginning there was counterfeit money. In the end there was a long queue at the fish 'n' chip shop where the staff were holding £20 notes to the light and making everybody feel uncomfortable scrutinising the notes and tearing at the silver foil. You patted yourself on the back if it was alright. No chips, but the bum's rush if your laser photocopy didn't pass the test.

London Film-makers Co-op has been at it for many decades and visiting their Gloucester Avenue hide-out can be an enriching experience. Once a month they show films by all comers and this time I saw some admirable film animation work by absolute beginners. We were also shown a film purportedly made by the Ministry of Art (military section) about "the dream cognicity of bereaved twins". This is recommended showing at cinemas – certificate A.

On the subject of censorship, newspapers and other media editors are supposed to be leaned upon by the authorities and served with what is called D (Don't mention) Notice. But how is news controlled? I would like to hear from subscribers who live outside London as to how many readers were aware of the fact that for the past three days a mass eviction of homeless by the Ministry of Transport was taking place in Leytonstone (in the proclaimed republic of Wandstonia). Those who listened to BBC radio listened in vain.

L*i* (power) and *min* (people), when simply put together in the Chinese language as *min li*, signifies 'people's power'. Using additional significant words in this monosyllabic language in various positions, various meanings are achieved. The syllable *ta* (you'll be pleased to hear) can be a noun, adjective, verb, what you will. *Ta* means great, greatness, to be great and thank you very much. But to continue with *min li*, by adding it to the syllable *y* it comes to mean *y min li*, employ people's power.

O*di et amo, quare id faciam, fortasse requiris. Nescio, sed fieri sentio et escrucior.* Catullus wrote the above to explain the unexplainable, the emotions aroused by the terrible twins of love and hate. Although Latin was the ruler's language, the slaves were the scribes and many of their locked-in thoughts are discernible.

Going backwards and forwards in time to examples takes less time than actual travel. Shakespeare four hundred years ago (in 1594) published *Richard III* with its famous cry: "A horse, a horse, my kingdom for a horse" which still sounds to me anarchist economics at its best.

Yet Shakespeare's language was anything but decorous. Here is Richmond exulting over his slain foe: "The day is ours, the bloody dog is dead."

A correspondent has chided me for not having treated the War Office with more respect in recent articles. I am told, and concede, that the War Office is still the greatest textile manufacturer in the world since 1914 and have made enough khaki to put a girdle round the world six or seven times over.

10th December 1994

Last year I made two resolutions. One was not to read anything else other than the anarchist press. The second, that after a year of abstention I would make a review of the mass circulated newspapers.

I am pleased to say that I have kept to the first resolution throughout the year and benefited enormously having lived on this, so to speak, healthy diet. The time, which otherwise would have been spent on reading the unreadable press, I could now spend on reading the works of authors I have long since neglected.

But the second resolution I'm unable to keep. I have no intention, and I am certainly not in the mood, to wade through a year's production of the world's newspapers in order to assimilate all the garbage accomplished last year. This resolution anyway was meant for 1994 and only now do I notice a contradiction in terms. How could I review in the same year of 1994 the newspapers I haven't read, for if I did that would have broken my first resolution. A lucky escape and a poor defence, but I'm glad of it.

As it happens I'm seriously thinking of giving up even listening to what is derisorily called the news on radio. Radio Three, which is just about obtainable on my set, in its news summary last night gave seven short items not including the weather (a good stand-by). As to be expected, none of the news was worth hearing: three of the items were fed in by the police, two by the army via the Foreign Office, one incomprehensible item from the US about something that either happened or will happen in Washington and, to acknowledge some home listeners agog for the news, there was an item about the Lottery which is now acknowledged to be the most successful tax increase through the back door in years. Why should anyone listen to such rubbish?

Never have there been tighter controls on what constitutes news. During the three-day evictions of the M11 protesters the news from Leytonstone was a conveniently produced police atrocity story, the only concession to audibility were short mentions on transport news where motorists were advised to avoid the area.

Even London Transport – management, union and workers – have cooperated in the evictions with the police and the bailiffs by closing down local underground stations in order to restrict the number of supporters arriving to support the protesters.

Readers may also remember that when Joy Gardner died the anti-establishment sentiment which swept the country was only broken by the 'news' of a refugee child arriving here from Bosnia, at the personal instigation of the Prime Minister, which swept the story under the carpet.

Here is a quote from some of the books I bagged: "Some writing is the repetition of the pleasure of seeing a thought unfurl as letters follow each other, filling the empty page, how each thought is penned, so that years later self might meet self and cry or laugh about the content ... Imitation is natural to man from childhood, one of his advantage over the lower animals being this, that he is the most imaginative creature in the world and learns at first by imitation ...

The [full] explanation is to be found in a further fact: to be learning something is the greatest pleasure not only to the philosopher but also to the rest of mankind, however small their capacity for it ..." (Aristotle, translation by Ingram Bywater, 1920).

"When each gladness had gone, gathering sorrow may cloud the brain: and in his breast a man cannot then see how his sorrows shall end, *tea ofereode, thisses swa maeg* ...

Yet that passed over; this may too" (translation by Michael Alexander, the Lament of Deor from early English writing).

Or as the early Spanish used to say, *Non pasaran*.

14th January 1995

As anarchist circles are getting more numerous, gone are the early days when it was possible to have most of the activists within the confines of one or two meeting rooms.

Anarchist literature reflected the necessities. Most articles concerned themselves with outside events, drawing attention to difficult situations in remote parts of the country where a show of solidarity was needed. It was not unusual to see the London Anarchist Group banner (does anybody know what happened to it?) in Faslane or the Glasgow Anarchist Group's banner in Whitehall. They were there fluttering from all parts of the country and from abroad (the FIJL's in particular). Where the flags fluttered they always achieved something. Some encroachment was made not to succeed, some concession, however small, was gained, perhaps they opened the jail doors for somebody. My favourite banner was the Oxford Anarchist Group's (do they still exist?). Most flags were black or red, Oxford's was a pinky blue.

The marches achieved a lot and comradeship was tremendous. Authority did not have it all its own way.

It can never be estimated what was the effect of worldwide protest against the Vietnam war.

The Aldermaston marches started with one man sitting down in the middle of Whitehall, his placard brought out a cordon of police. The following year there were hundreds od protesters.

Even the manner of finding out about the Aldermaston secret atomic establishment showed how one observant person cut across the veil of secrecy perpetrated by government and their lips-sealed stooges.

The man was a bus-spotter and he noticed a bus, ordinary London Transport bus, with a number which was unknown to him. He followed this bus out of curiosity and ended up in Aldermaston and saw with his own eyes this fenced-up horror story.

We all have brains and brawn (not to mention bairns). We can use both, either or none. There is honesty in all three.

There were also songs such as those quoted in *Visions of Poesy*. I don't know what the tune is to Paul Goodman's 'Flags, 1967' – "... my black flag the sovereignty of no man or law!" – but if you play it I'll sing it.

Visions of Poesy is dotted with references to the black flag. You may look at George Woodcock's, which is the final poem in the book. For me the flag is no more than a symbol, a presence, a warning, but as the poet says (and he should know): "For out of black / soul's night have stirred / dawn's cold gleam / morning;s singing bird."

The contribution of the anarchist movement is of historic importance and our record on civil rights, in the defence of communities, in defeating and in the organisation against oppressive laws, speaks for itself.

Today the movement is stretched, spread out to its limits. For those who say there has never been an anarchist society I'd say there have been many colonies of anarchists who have stayed together, despite the change of generation, for almost a hundred years. It is only a question of size, but even in my own lifetime I have noted that anarchism in practice is both enduring and liberating.

There is no other movement in the country or anywhere in the world which operates as does the anarchist, openly, spontaneously and altruistically. We do not resign to superstition, bigotry, chauvinism of any kind. We are not afraid of power, neither master nor slave.

28th January 1995

London anarchists have been wondering if a day could be set aside for a communal get-together of the population. In past years, and for historical reasons, May Day was usually chosen. I remember attending such a march from Tower Hill to Victoria Park organised by Workers Mutual Aid, when the slogan was May Day is Workers Day. But, as Kropotkin could have pointed out, in these latitudes the beginning of May is a bit chilly and damp for a picnic. The suggestion is then to hold the gatherings in future about the middle of June when the sun is at its greatest potential voltage and many such festive congregations could grace a convenient beanfield. It was about ten years ago that reaction was at its most savage and brutal, when of course the families of miners and printworkers were defeated and the convoy was smashed in one particular beanfield.

In the meantime (and a mean time it is) what is proposed is a walk through picturesque scenery.

Might is still right (even if the latest lot is only best at irritating). One law replaces another, and *both* are continued to be used. None of these laws, hastily written to satisfy demand, are anything approaching natural law. In the old days the law pretended to be virtuous. Immorality was not a fit source for taxation. Now they wish to bring criminal business under the same roof, as long as the state gets its share as well.

Injustice is unequal justice. The law now wishes to curtail the movement of the population in the minutest way. The law stands that should you walk down, however peacefully, any public pathway you can now be challenged by a person in appropriate fancy dress and told not to proceed. Disobeying such an injunction means instant arrest, bother and expense. Ever since the Falklands war, when the term exclusion zone made the dictionaries, such zones have been devised by our lawmakers. There are fences put up by property and privilege through which you may not pass. Not through common land, not down by the riverside or up the mountain or down to the seashore.

Through this land you may not pass. Why not? 'It's orders. *They* pay my wages, not *you*, sir.' 'Is that all?' 'That's all sir, now move along or otherwise I'll have to arrest you.' 'Arrest me! What for?' 'Never mind the what for, just move along.'

Authoritarian law is the codified will of the rulers. There are extenuating circumstances for the wickedest crimes against humanity. The rulers are above the law.

This is the malaise, comrades, and the cure is obvious to all who have been living in the shelter of the anarchist movement. Perhaps the only defence is the sharing of resources.

Including the law.

One indication of the overall repression is the curtailment through the law and brutal powers of free gatherings and festivals. All the attempts last year have failed.

Now is the time, comrades, to prove that the law is an ass. Or perhaps wait until June, when the sun is at its height.

Solstice at midsummer at Stonehenge, would you say that would be a suitable place for a picnic?

11th February 1995

Recently I spent a considerable time (yet another bonus of not reading the gutter press) studying the works of Thomas Kyd, the Elizabethan dramatist who is probably most admired for *The Spanish Tragedy*. I was fortunate enough to peruse the 1592 edition printed by Edward Allde, for Edward White. Alas, the name of the author is not revealed. It is only through scholarly surmise, even innuendo, that one of the best playwrights has a name at all. Similarly to Shakespeare, *not a single line of his writing in his own hand remains* and the only scrap of evidence that he existed at all is a clumsily written description of the contents of his desk, which he shared with Christopher Marlowe, after his chambers were raided by the police spy, and this 'evidence' I have also seen.

Elizabeth I, Good Queen Bess, was a monarch controlled by her secret police and even tricked into policies by Walsingham, head of the snooping department. Letters forged by him led to the execution of Babington and his followers and then subsequently to the killing of Mary Queen of Scots. A recent article in *Freedom* attacks the republican Cromwell for the suppression of Catholics in Ireland. Cromwell inherited the situation. The first blame must go to the secret police and Walsingham, for it managed to sever the reconciliation of religious groupings during a period of great cultural distinction and comparative tolerance. To bring the matter into perspective awaits the anarchist historian, but it should be mentioned at this stage that Elizabeth I was not an absolute monarch, that her hand was forced by her manipulators and clearly she had to live with the knowledge that her father, Henry VIII, when Elizabeth was three years old, engineered the killing of her own mother.

Strange as it may seem, that period of enlightenment left no manuscripts by Thomas Kyd, who nevertheless is credited with numerous plays. It is also asserted that Kyd wrote poetry. F.S. Boas in his *The Works of Thomas Kyd* mentions (page xxv) that there is still extant in the British Museum "what may be a specimen of his non-dramatic hack work". It is a slim pamphlet printed by John Wolfe back in 1586 which contains three stanzas written by Chidioth Tychborne on the eve of his execution (Tychborne and six others, including Babington, ascended the bloody scaffold on 20th September 1586). There is a virtuous answer to Tychborne's poem on the opposing page entitled 'Hendecassyllabon T.K. in Cygneam Cantionem'. Boas thought 'T.K.' could read for Thomas Kyd because some of the phrases are ones "of which Kyd is fond" such as "thy hope, thy hap and all" and also "time trieth trueth and trueth hath reason tript" and echoes of both phrases are to be found in Kyd's authenticated works. This verified answer is certainly the work of a hack, a practised hand who can certainly turn out the ringing phrase and to whom it matters little whose side he may hurt or praise.

E ven here the past is obscure. Kyd himself is a mystery, perhaps the author of an early very popular version of *Hamlet*. No copy remains. It would take a lifetime's devotion to unravel the facts. How much was lost in that police raid will never be known. But this poem, so-called, is T.K.'s own fault, nobody else's. Tychborne says (and I find his poem moving): "My thread is cut, and yet it is not spunne". T.K. venemously replies: "Thy ill spent youth thine after yeares hath nipt, / And God that saw thee hath preserude our Queen, / Her thread still holds, thine perisht though unspun, / And she shall live when traitors lives are done."

A pamphlet produced in 1964 which purports to be a copy of Tychborne's elegy and T.K.'s answer, although handsomely produced needs yet to be "corrected and amended of such grosse faults as passed in the first impression". The 1586 original is in the British Museum, a forerunner of the gutter press, decorously printed.

R evenge personified is the theme of *The Spanish Tragedy* and is given utterance in the words of humans. The concept does not allow for the acknowledgement of emotion. This idea is now alien to us, a concept we can hardly contemplate. Through the thickening of our *alma mater* the voice of bygone ages hardly penetrates at all.

C hidioth Tychborne has no entry in that usually most reliable *Dictionary of English Literature* (W. Davenport Adams) and I haven't found any other example of his work. As to why human beings collectively both try to preserve *and* destroy all proofs of achievements has puzzled me more than anything else. The manifold brain of humanity had so many knocks from left and right that I shudder to think what will be our heritage when the anarchist reason will at last shine upon us all.

H elped by my own knowledge of poetry nevertheless, and the way of gutter journalism, I think I can elucidate a little on Boas's contention, disregarded by and large for the past ninety years, that the poem referred to above may well have been written by Thomas Kyd. I am trying to be generous to T.K. but from observation many

examples could be quoted where a response to an existing poem is in
fact a compliment. T.K.'s language and answer is vicious but the title
'Hendecassyllabon T.K. in Cygneam Cantionem Chidrochi –
Tychborne' is a gentle touch. Remember this is, in modern terms, a
Samizdat publication – Walsingham's police had to be taken into
consideration. The title is a swan-song in eleven syllables (to a line).
Swans were supposed to sing most sweetly before they died.
Tychborne was the last to die and in the manner of his death – he was
hung, then taken down while still alive and chopped into little pieces
with the quartering knife, into eleven pieces – like a line of eleven
syllables.

25th February 1995

Perhaps the first thing to mention is that luckily I've found time to attend Norman Bacrac's illustrated lectures on natural science. Mr Bacrac is the present editor of the *Ethical Record*, a consistently interesting monthly journal which mainly contains written texts of the wide range of talks at the Conway Hall. The lectures were given in the Ethical Society's time-honoured library, excellent surroundings in which to be reminded of the marvellous theories of science, looked at from a humanist point of view, and take stock of past and present scientific activities.

However few its manifestations, the ground is still held by humanist science, just about. Science, of course, is free even if some scientists are in chains and few are on unlimited expense accounts.

Yet I could never entirely distinguish between scientific games and experimental science and I wonder why it is so that the most profound scientific definitions click out of the human brain using the language of fairy tales, for example the ancient riddle of the snake swallowing its own tail that came to F.A. Kekule in a dream which suggested to him the graphic representation of the benzene ring.

Sometimes formulas have to be understood, sometimes experiments must be made. But then who harnesses all this knowledge and for what ends? Has there been really so much progress, when ten long moons ago our ancestors had a leephone with its own distinctive pitch which could be heard for miles. What technology! Just a cunningly shaped wood slung round on a string with an outstretched hand. Whoever worked out the right proportions for that gadget could have been amused by Heisenberg's Uncertainty Principle.

Important to take these things into consideration during a period of most intense technological strivings whose cost is astronomical and whose benefits are illusory. There has never been a dearer cost of living in any period of human history. Modifications of technology just for the sake of modifications, as Colin Ward pointed out recently, are nothing but a nuisance. I also would like to have a *better* typewriter not a *different* type of machine, although I still prefer to write my articles by hand and only then to type the whole thing out, modifying where it may be necessary.

Capitalism, as readers have been told before, is only interested in profit. It may not have occurred to anybody before but the painstakingly put together table of elements from Actinium to

Zirconium, all 104 of them at the last time of counting, figure prominently in the Dow-Jones Index. Possibly Adrian Mitchell's famous lines "Most people don't take notice of most poetry because most poetry don't take notice of most people" could apply to some scientists as well.

Salus populi suprema lex esto – let the welfare of the people be the final law. Those who call themselves scientists could use the old phrase as their guiding principle.

11th March 1995

No change can be observed in the human being since written records and drawings have been kept for many thousands of years. Neither the size nor the ability, bodily or mentally, has altered. What the early writers have written can be read today without much difficulty and you shall find that the subjects and problems have not changed one iota. It is for this reason that I find reading ancient writers so interesting.

What I cannot understand is how, despite all warnings by the wisest, the human condition has remained the same. In other words progress, if any, has been slow. Political conditions, or conditioning, has not altered. The rulers are few and change their guises. While all our efforts are spent on restraining the foe at home, the conditions deteriorate abroad.

There are seven million people *homeless* in the richest country in the world. You do not know, you are not told, but even if you know there is nothing that you can do about it.

There is a dialogue extant of which I am reminded between the poet Horace (very much the anarchist) and a lawyer who advises Horace not to write satires but to write Caesar's praise or otherwise *keep quiet*. Says the lawyer: "When the mighty passion of poetry is upon you, you poor wretch, venture to sing the exploits of invincible Caesar; you will gain many rewards for your labours."

Nothing has changed. When you follow the dictates of the ruling club it's roses, roses all the way. But thousands of years later one is grateful to Horace because all his life is still open to our view, as he wished it, "painted on votive tablet".

Who else had the good sense to write down and respect the thoughts of his slave Davus: "Who then is free? He who is wise, over himself true lord and unterrified by anything that passes." A modern reminder is when the atom bomb was described as a paper tiger.

But things have changed in the methods of rulers in the past half century. Writing itself has become an anachronism in itself. A recent proof of this is the august BBC which will not commission 'new writing' this year. The message only denotes the source. Murdoch's monster screens flickering images from Peking to Athens, the picture images of basketball players, there is no language except noise, the roaring of the crowd, the smack of the ball into the net, new kinds of educators have taken over. Now what should be understood has a different meaning to what needs to be understood. As long as you learn how to tie your shoelaces, that should give you an easy honours degree. The bad drives out the good is an old saying, but the logic of it is only now being understood. For if all knowledge is trivia then you might as well sit in front of your monster screen and watch the illusion of movement. A scriptwriter working for these people, before being sacked, managed to change the script aiming at total incomprehension, such as: "Zybesco just won the shot put with a toss of minus eight feet."

Ever since the '60s, which gave the ruling class its worst shock worldwide, the tactics have changed. By definition the 'subjects' are those who are in your grip. The communication satellites, those big lamps shining into everybody's homes and into public places, you just watch, and they are the final modifications in control and power. In the old days the poor king had to send his messengers around with the symbol of a bloody sword whereas today's messengers will show you nothing that you need to know, but they do teach two or three words of English and how to open your mouth for your shouts of joy and sorrow.

The advocates of electronic mail could put this into their pipe and smoke it that when the method of subjugation is 'to push the buttons of meaninglessness and see who jumps' the only revolutionary answer is to switch off. When three satellites, equally spaced around the globe, is all that is needed for total control of all communications, can you imagine what the Anarchist Broadcasting Corporation would put out to astound its worldwide audience?

25th March 1995

W hat's the news? Some maintain that news as such is impartial; the retelling of some event which is of some interest. On this score almost anything or everything is news, even little Johnnie's bellyache.

News is all things worth remembering or taking into account. Something that the individual and all other individuals need to remember and should take into account, so the news of the day is everything that needs to be remembered and to be taken into account. Even the pimple on Johnnie's or Tony's neck. I've got a bigger pimple on my neck, says Johnnie. This is where Tony protests, that the news really is the pimple on his neck. If there is any other news, it can be safely forgotten. This of course is an absurdity, for tomorrow all which has been 'ignored' today will have to be remembered. At your peril that you or Johnnie forgets the pimple on his neck.

So news – which old readers may remember I've stopped reading in favour of *Freedom* and other anarchist literature – cannot be all the news, just a sample.Come the anarchist millennium, a new definition for what constitutes news will have to be found. There is no doubt in my mind that trivia will still have the greatest circulation, but then little Johnnie's appetite for trivia will be no longer a major concern.

News is of constituent parts answering routine questions (what, when, where, who, which, why, etc.) with four types of answers: a) nothing, b) nothing new, c) something unusual, d) something extraordinary. Over the waters the fifth type of answer – 'You don't say' – is invariably added.

So when Oscar Wilde was asked at American customs '*What* have you got to declare?' he had every right to declare '*Nothing* [category a)] but my genius [category d)]'. And it has been news ever since.

Usually when the answer to the question 'What happened?' is 'Nothing' it can still be category d), for all things may be expected to happen so if nothing took place how did that happen, or even not happen.

However, the meaning behind the laconic answer 'Nothing' may be understood as '*Everything continues as before and as expected*, there is nothing to report'. When there is a slight alteration it produces a new development, something unheard of or unconsidered before, and the mention of it is a small indication of its news content, c). However, the billions of human activities, although individually of equal importance, are discounted in favour of a short range of samples such as Johnnie's pimple revelation, or anything else which passes for thought in editorial circles.

So there you are, sitting in your editorial chair, sitting by your cosy fire, and you choose the item for your all important front page. Without a doubt you will disregard any others but what you yourself think will interest, grab your ever grateful readers. Perhaps some photograph of pollution of the sunset in the west, still visible. Or a rather murkier view of a busy street in Bangkok at noon where the traffic lights are not visible ten yards away. Guess which of the two would sell more copies.

For me, the news of the week was the bicyclists stopping the traffic in Piccadilly, cheered by an enthusiastic crowd in the Circus.

It is a good news hunch to go for the story the other papers ignore to push the latest bit of policy.

So remember, as you tie your shoelaces, it could be the news of the week, pushing Johnnie's pimple off the front page and into the dustbins of history.

8th April 1995

Warily the anarchist watches as the pent-up emotions come to the fore. Individuals and communities suddenly see a chink of light. The poorest of the poor among us band together, find comradeship, shelter, food and good company. It is unbelievable that side by side of ostentatious wealth and riches such a layer of consistent poverty should exist in this advanced capitalist country. That the self-appointed, or even anointed, executive is making heavy weather of the distribution of undoubted wealth, surely the easiest task of all, has resulted in pitiful lives overall of individuals and communities. This is a world of infinite surplus, renewable through harvest and birth both of working power and materials. Everything is usable and adaptable. But the system, the ruling system vaguely described as capitalism, whether private or of the state, is in itself an incoherent concoction with its built-in crises and unavoidable wars and contradictions and confrontations. Everything is free, but the false rhetoric enforced by the clubs, the enormous clubs, of the law ensure that everything has a price. This is all engineered by the self-appointed executive with their sham elections, for the rules of the elections are laid down by the executive and the rules are so constructed that only the people who are in power stay in power. So why hasn't the whole caboodle been sent packing a long time ago? The problem is that however absurd the system, once it is foisted on a population which has no choice but to endure living under it, worse through the efforts of the same population, will totter on indefinitely. In this world of persistent surplus no system, however incoherent, however despotic, however vicious, can or will be seen to fail completely. The four year old children weaving your carpets for a rupee a day, the thousands of unpaid mining your copper at gunpoint are, in terms of capitalism, only an economic entry and signal that the system works, even if the soap is made from the bones and skins of the holocaust victims. The shareholders ought to be pleased.

A certain kind of elation is however observable which seems to permeate the whole of society from Brightlingsea to the Orkneys. Communal experiments are entered into with tremendous energy and are seen to succeed on an ever-increasing scale. In my own locality alone anarchist ideas are becoming common currency. How it is happening nobody quite knows, for the formal copybook anarchist is practically non-existent.

It is nonetheless a very dangerous period and our best hope still remains that by now, through some curious system of political osmosis, there are enough anarchists in place in all professions, trades and interest groups whose combined wisdom and weight as citizens of influence can stand up to the counter-weight of the doctrinaire executive.

There are no difficulties unsolvable in a functioning anarchist society. The only requirement remaining is the need for sovereign individuals, in Lionel Bart's immortal words: "Consider yourself part of the furniture", to accept the simple tenet that the welfare of the community it all inclusive.

In this material world human beings are beginning to realise that co-operation and mutual aid and a say in what is needed to produce is a thousand times more efficient than the hit and miss methods of capitalism. Yet of course only the highest and most advanced societies practice mutual aid. Without such wisdom the population perishes.

Nevertheless, there are enough hidey-holes for those involved in purely their private pursuits, and these might not wish to abandon these same pursuits just for the sake of an abstract idea: the good of the community. Let the anarchists remind others and themselves that nobody can survive the first years of their childhood without the constant care and attention, dare I mention love, of their fellows.

Group thinking has always been difficult. As you know to your cost, most models of organisation have the smell of prison about them, and the simple and the innocent, the person of good will, is always proved to be wrong. Times are a-changing. At the push of the button you may now switch off the system. Fair enough. As long as you push the right button. Philip Sansom used to say that you cannot have an anarchist society without a society of anarchists. There is no fear, except the word fear itself. We live in a world of free materials and of free labour. We have made this country at best described as an open prison. The population is groping towards anarchy. Don't let them be fobbed off with some capitalist lookalike.

29th April 1995

Land is the big issue

Whenever possible I try to take part in some communal activity which by its very nature has something to do with anarchist principles. The recent land occupation exercise in Surrey was such an occasion. It turned out to be very successful, heartening and more than symbolic event. In many respects it once again proved, if it needs proving at all, that anarchist organisation based on voluntary co-operation achieves wonders. The organisers' main aim was to call for a universal right of access to uncultivated land in the countryside.

Land is now a very big issue. Not only are vast tracts of land 'set-aside' but various government departments, from the military to 'health' departments, have vast land possessions for which they have no use whatsoever. By the dictates of the system of monopoly capitalism these lands are held back, for if they were put up for sale land values could decline sharply and would completely knock out the already shaky property markets.

The government, if there is such a thing, is in a quandary. It was their privatisation policy which has created the situation by which the nationalised industries now privatised are in a queue trying to sell off surplus land. A hundred thousand acres here, a million acres there. If all that land is sold at once, even you and I could buy an acre for the odd shilling. This is where monopoly restrictions are the only safeguard for their corrupt system and this is why a 'back to the land' movement has become such a threat to the establishment.

But this eventual unstoppable disposal of land held by the various government departments and of the military, coupled with the set-aside policy of land by monopoly capitalism, may well pave the way for the greatest distribution of land that will break the power of centuries of enclosures.

For it is the very tenets of privatisation which will hoist them with their own petard, these vast tracts of land which they are unwilling to dispose of yet have no use for whatsoever.

The site which was finally chosen for the land occupation was a vast and disused airfield at Wisley, a piece of land in present economic terms of little value and which does not seem to have been put to any use whatsoever.

On arrival we could at once see how efficient and successful are the anarchist colonies. The main driving force was the admirable Donga tribe who have refined the art of combining earth skills of the past with whatever is sensible in the new technology.

When we arrived a camp had already been set up showing all the familiar features of the modern anarchist village. Benders galore, tents, wooden lodges, tree-houses and in the middle a circular leafy geodesic dome for communal discussion. Even anarchists march on their stomachs and there was the most amazing kitchen capable of providing free wholesome food, with second helpings, for the 300 people. There was even a sweat lodge and even a hot bath with two taps for cold and hot next to the gently gurgling stream. Other wonders included a sculptural masterpiece of an earth oven for baking bread.

The information lodge was full of leaflets of similar events, occupations, appeals for help from all over the country. The front page of the local Surrey paper was very appreciative of the land occupation, quoting local farmers fully supporting the movement, "after all, why shouldn't the land be put to proper use?"

A patch of land was carefully dug and prepared for planting, and here again there were many local people giving a hand. This made me understand once again that authority is just another name for people working together and taking for granted their right to do so. There is no doubt whatsoever that anarchism is also a return to the land movement and we are all descendants of dispossessed peasants.

Bela Bartok, dying in poverty and of malnutrition in New York, recalled that the oath a peasant most feared was the old mother cursing her unloving son in these words: "For your callous indifference to me and mine may you be reduced in your old age to the buying of your own bread". Indeed, the bitter bread of exile is nothing compared to the humiliation of always being dependent on other people's charity.

The authorities are unwilling to release the expropriated land for the simple reason that if all land was sold the market would collapse.

The land is the common treasury of all, so sang the Diggers and it was appropriate that we should go to St George's Hill and there see written, performed and enacted a play, compellingly written and acted in faultless rhyme and imagery, the historical pageant of oppression by state and church of the people through the ages who are finally liberated by the natural spirits of anarchy. It was the best open air play I have ever seen, marvellously acted in the best

Shakesperian tradition. Idyllic surroundings, even if the historic spot is now a golf course and even if that finale of dance and merriment was drowned out by the noise of Concorde flying right above the hill with all the noise of an outdated technology reminding all the assembled of unfinished business.

13th May 1995

For several years in the '60s we used to have an anarchist platform in Hyde Park, sometimes even two. No doubt it was a circus and most of the audience came to see the speakers making fools of themselves. Those with the loudest voices usually attracted the largest crowds, but every experienced speaker knew that without hecklers the crowds were thin. Some of the hecklers were more knowledgeable than the speakers and some experienced listeners followed the hecklers round getting enjoyment out of the havoc they were able to cause. One of the chief hecklers was an anarchist himself, very ready with dates and facts and could quote long passages from anarchist writers and was inordinately pleased with himself as the crowd grew into a multitude around the anarchist soap-box. It was due to the sharp wit and repartee of the exchanges and the audience loved the drama. A really brilliant speaker when confronted with more than one heckler could pick and choose which one to answer. What he had to watch against was the hecklers completely taking over the meeting, the audience deserting the speaker completely. The memory of these people was astounding. "You are contradicting yourself, they'd say, or "Kropotkin never said that" or "Emma would be ashamed of you".

Now that we are returning to Speakers' Corner, no doubt the situation has changed drastically. But, for the spreading of anarchist ideas, a public meeting is invaluable. Not only many thousands listen to you with attention, but what you say will surface in everyday conversations at home, in the workplace or wherever. Here was also a chance to sell anarchist literature at the gates and many people afterwards attended the meetings in the evening organised by the London Anarchist Group, which has since sunk without trace although it was very lively and influential in those days.

There is something about the human voice and the interchange of ideas which can be very liberating for both speaker and audience alike. No doubt there is the feeling of the market- place about it, but here you can hear the *vox populi* and many writers hung up with their syntax would benefit from such raw exposure. The crowd is made up of individuals and when it comes to question time the queries come thick and fast, asking what then is the anarchist point of view. In those days I was probably better informed by just listening to the crowd than reading any number of newspapers.

The effect of regularly speaking at Hyde Park, especially on the anarchist platform, gave one without doubt an audience of which any well-known actor would be proud. Not a day would pass without somebody stopping you in the street with "Hey, I know you" or giving you the thumbs-up sign for no reason at all.

Of course speaking at Hyde Park is speaking in the shadow of the Tynburn gallows, thereby continuing a quaint tradition. Those condemned to die were allowed to make their final speeches with the crowds gaping at them and by tradition you may set up your stall at any such place – at Tower Hill, for example, and in Manette Street just by Foyles in Charing Cross Road, where I remember an anarchist meeting so large at the time of the Cuban crisis in 1962 that the crowds were standing in the middle of Charing Cross Road and the traffic had to be diverted.

I also remember that one of the most successful public meetings which were held in Hyde Park took place in 1968 when members of the London Anarchist Group II kept up a marathon speak-in for thirteen days, basically to stop the war in Vietnam, but also to spread the ideas of anarchism. The crowds were vast and appreciative. One of the speakers was Bob Dylan and Joan Baez sang a song for peace. Even the hecklers applauded.

27th May 1995

L and is the big issue. I notice that the excellent and inspiring *Scottish Anarchist* (welcome, welcome, a thousand times welcome) in an article on the uses of the electronic reference library notes that certain anarchist subjects and causes are well represented. Could someone type in the Land Registry? We cannot have an anarchist society until we know how much land is available or, in common parlance, how the land lies.

A narchists are the only people who have a proper respect for the past. Thomas More was right to say that cursed be who removes a single stone from the edifice of knowledge. I was recently reminded that all that remains of the little town of Lidice is a memorial stone in the London Borough of Hackney. The Nazis come in many guises. The worst tale I've heard recently was of the all-triumphant collective farm where the director pointed proudly around him: "This was once a mere village".

N ews travels slowly. I read in the June 1995 issue of that lovingly conscientious trade union paper the *Industrial Worker* (now in its 92nd year) that an International Trades Union Congress was held in Kathmandu, Nepal, last December. One of the subjects discussed by the delegates (among them the AIT and the Swedish AC) was the modern slavery of the 'Free Trade Zones' which have been installed all over Asia, where the so-called 'trans- nationals' enjoy complete control, and where of course unions are not allowed. There was strong interest in syndicalism among the delegates and the wording of the Kathmandu Declaration has strong echoes of old fashioned wobbly language.

G eorge Woodcock, who died recently, received two long pages of obituaries in *Freedom*. I see in the current *Drunken Boat* (a thoroughly good read even if the art, good as it is, needs to be better printed – a smudge is a smudge is a smudge) lurking on the back pages was a vicious attack on *Freedom*, this very same courageous periodical which has never wavered in either quality or in its advocacy of anarchism. Woodcock wrote this piece, unrelenting in his dying months, and it is incomprehensible to me how he could have taken this stand. Woodcock thought that *Freedom* had declined in the '60s when, in my biased opinion, it was as good as could be with limited resources. Woodcock was not the only intellectual who queried this trend but, as I now see from *Drunken Boat*, he was the most precise.

Good of *Drunken Boat* to print it for now we know the exact cause of his indignation: "*Freedom* declined in quality over the years", he says, and adds "and nowadays seem to condescend to the workers who are supposed to be the majority of their readers". I wish they still did, but many of them through reading *Freedom* have become university professors.

U ntiring in my efforts to educate myself, I have also had the pleasure to look at another anarchist paper, *Anarchy – A Journal of Desire Armed,* which convinces me that our comrades over there have either a larger movement or more spondulicks at their disposal. I still prefer the poverty-stricken style of the old (Colin Ward's) *Anarchy* with its real art covers by Rufus Segar which contained few articles, none of them souped up yet each of them memorable. Perhaps I'm infected by the local reserve, but I can't see why conciseness is not admired.

A bolish water charges! *Workers Solidarity*, the Irish anarchist paper, is big and bright and campaigns in direct language. The Federation of Dublin Anti-Water Charge Campaign has a very great following and its strategy includes that not just every court case will be contested but hear the voice of the true anarchist: "Where water is disconnected, reconnection will be arranged!"

G reat is my relief to read in the current *Ethical Record* a note by Erskine Childers on the cost of the United Nations system worldwide, excluding the World Bank and IMF staff and peace-keeping troops, with a mere 51,500 personnel, they only receive eight billion dollars a year – which in this writer's opinion is what the great British public spends on alcohol in six months. To turn the argument on its head, should the UN staff be paid in alcohol instead?

E very job has its compensations, but when you are working you cannot also be on every action. My comrades are well on their way to Stonehenge now, some by boat, some on foot, towards an exclusion zone. What efforts this so-called government exerts to stop people contemplating their ancient heritage. Keep cool and watch your tongue – it could be you.

10th June 1995

Venturous as ever, *Freedom*'s editorial writer proposes an anarchist international newspaper. Would we have the resources for such an enterprise? That's not all. A newspaper first and foremost needs journalists and an understanding of the constantly changing mode of reading 'the mobile weather systems'. Although the head of the London School of Journalism is an anarchist, his school has not turned out anarchist journalists. Freedom Bookshop has an extensive stock of anarchist journals which appear periodically, and brave efforts they are, but nobody could claim them to be newspapers.

In an anarchist society news as such will have to be redefined. Births, deaths, marriages – will they still be front-page news? Earthquakes, disasters, floods, failure of harvests. Clearly it will be a peaceful society and prosperous, so all the news about wars, civil conflict, terrorism, gun-law, terrified refugees, will become a thing of the past. All news would become a celebration of life, the stressing of the value of mutual aid, altruism – would there still be a need for direct action? And will there still be a need for the consistent reiteration of editorial reason, pointing at the precipice, the warning voice against the great slide backwards?

Out of human suffering, the poet said, come the years that bring the philosophic mind.

Looking at the present day anarchist papers there is little to distinguish them from their capitalist counterparts. Those which use the tabloid methods gain a wider readership, but I doubt that the language they use frightens anybody any more than the conscientious anarchist reader. Their rejoicing when the odd enemy of the people gets his just deserts may work up the tribal spirit more than cogent advocations of anarchist principles.

Even so, we have to deal with the present when a regular anarchist news-sheet would be more than welcome. Can you imagine what the headline on the front-page would be of today's issue – perhaps 'Mass Demonstration Against Nuclear Testing'? Even if the accompanying photo would show only six people and a dog.

Not an easy matter. For the anarchist dawn is not yet here. The papers are full of atrocities. If you look at the local papers you can see how much their content and circulation depends on what the courts and the police dish out. Every second story is one of horror: 'Man lying critically ill was struck on head by a heavy metal place dropped on his head from a railway bridge' – no, his name was not Chirac. Three stories of people having been knifed for inconsiderable sums of money. The wrong car blown up in a revenge attack.

Clearly, comrades, we won't have this sort of behaviour in an anarchist society where reason and consideration for others will prevail, where there'll be no 'haves' and 'have-nots', where not only the individual has become sane but so has society itself.

Eventually the time will come when the flapping ears of the dog outside the French Embassy in London will have stopped the atomic tests in Tahiti. Until then there is a lot of work to do, and an international anarchist newspaper would be a great help as well as intellectual dynamite.

24th June 1995

I cannot review *Visions of Poesy*, for I have contributed to it. Nevertheless, I hope that a proper assessment will appear in *Freedom* one day, for I think it is an excellent compilation. There are seventy poets included and it is a treasure store, a good book to browse through.With a novel or other type of fiction it is easier to deal with in a review. With poetry it is a more personal matter. Something jumps off the page and sticks in your mind. To give you a few examples:

"we want / to put to music and truth / in our underwear" (**Julian Beck**)

"justice comes to those who take it, / not to those who wait" (**Boffo**)

"I'm an anarchist same as you when you are telephoning, turning on/off lights, drinking water" (**John Cage**)

"shall every official tongue be fried" (**Bryony Dahl**)

"their children, according to / the laws of heredity / one played the clarinet, one danced a minuet / and two were fortune tellers" (**Janet Dubé**)

"For wars will cease when men refuse to fight" (**Tom Earley**)

"Anarchy begin at the turnstile and the queue" (**Douglas Fetherling**)

"I am waiting for the age of anxiety to drop dead" (**Lawrence Ferlinghetti**)

"Who stole the Goose off the Common? / Who stole the Common of the Goose?"(**Dennis Gould**)

"I appoint Messrs Bakunin and Kropotkin my executors" (**Adrian Henri**)

"Laughter filled with sherbert fountains" (**Bernard Kops**)

"While our upper class Governors / lead lovely lives of crime" (**Tuli Kupferberg**)

"many poor people have to wait for their boxes" (**James Laughlin**)

"The offspring of flowers is a work of generations" (**Ursula Le Guin**)

"Words that may have the power / To make the sun rise again" (**Denise Levertov**)

"We have it here growing in our hearts" (**Philip Levine**)

"I think, am weak, need help, must live, / and will – with your permission – live" (**Christopher Logue**)

"Finally I was given the Chair of / Comparative Ambiguity" (**Adrian Mitchell**)

"gluing uncle Jim's false teeth / brought an end to all his shouting " (**Tom McSorley**)

"They didn't tell us what it would be like without trees"(**Tina Morris**)

"In rented rooms we mouth through dreams" (**Arthur Moyse**)

"When living resembles airport food" (**Marge Piercy**)

"I have waited to ask you this / I could not ask you in prison / I waited until you were free!" (**Paul Potts**)

"Ain't got no job / got what you deserve"(**Maxine Querty**)

"They marched five miles / carrying the black and scarlet banners"(**Herbert Read**)

"there is that land, oh land of the free / Don't say it never existed" (**J.R.**)

"What is it all for, this poetry / This bundle of accomplishment / Put together with so much pain?" (**Kenneth Rexroth**)

"Right now! Ah ha ha / ha ha! / 'Cos I wanna be anarchist / It's the only way to be!" (**Sex Pistols**)

"Plays oolya oolya to your bones" (**Michelle Shocked**)

"Why is life so difficult for my sons?" (**Monica Sjöö**)

"the sweet prairies of anarchy" (**Stevie Smith**)

"I must turn and go back: / caught on a snowpeak / between heaven and earth / And stand in lines in Seattle / looking for work" (**Gary Snyder**)

"Poets are a meagre species" (**Muriel Spark**)

"They accuse me of ras-ca-li-ty / Will the roses grow wild over me" (**T-Bone Slim**)

"underneath the asphalt / lies the tilth" (**Patricia V.T. West**)

"Let the black day die / Let the new day dawn"(**George Woodcock**)

And to end this anarchists dictionary of quotations with both by **anon**:

"Ova tannas Siam / Geeva tannas Siam / Ove tannas"

"Nineteenth century Spanish anarchist called their beliefs *The Idea*."

Right now! Ah ha ha ha ha ha!

                                                        8th July 1995

The previous article quoted a statement by John Cage, the composer who regarded intervals of silence between sounds as music, which said: "I'm an anarchist, same as you are when you're telephoning, turning on/off lights, drinking water". Even though Cage's idea is intellectually appealing, the situation is that today you are entirely in the hands of the suppliers of the service. Whereas the local supplier BT is claiming to cut the telephone bill by 5%, what they don't say is that you don't just pay for the calls but you also pay for the rental of both the equipment and the line. On top of that you also pay for a *tax on communication* – VAT at 17.5%, a government tax – so all in all there are a lot of things to attend to before you can call yourself a 'telephoning anarchist'. Let that go, for Cage's idea could come true overnight. For the time being, however, there is no such thing as a free service. Or more importantly a free access on demand to all its parts. There are, on the contrary, a list of services offered which intend to reduce free access.

The other week I also welcomed a suggestion for the publishing of 'Freedom International'. This is the context where some thought should be given to the telephone and radio systems which bring in the news internationally. How else would Reuters exist? To gather news for 'Freedom International' through the existing system based on profit would, even if the work was done entirely voluntarily, result in a colossal bill from the telephone company. Some instances of present prices: say, for example, the paper's reporters would spend ten minutes telephoning foreign parts, they would incur vastly different bills from their ever-loving Sid. You can tell by looking at the price list as to which are the poorest countries. They pay more. It is not a question of distance. To telephone the US or Canada costs £3.36 for ten minutes; to telephone Mexico will cost you £11.50; to telephone Northern Ireland is 84p; to telephone Southern Ireland is £2.43 for each ten minute conversation. These hefty sums are justified by BT simply as a reflection of foreign conditions, accessibility to satellites and safety of installations. The high price for a telephone call to Southern Ireland is justified by BT in that until recently telephone and other installations have been frequently blown up. Nevertheless you may telephone Northern Ireland for 84p, where presumably the telephone lines don't get blown up.

Here then is a great opportunity to start an internationally distributed paper, but you can imagine what an enormous undertaking it would be if done properly. Nevertheless, there is already a vigorous international section regularly printed in *Freedom*.

The word distribution is also a stumbling block. This paper alone ought to be better distributed, but 'International Freedom' will have to deal with the wholesalers of each of the 223 countries answerable by a telephone exchange, the likes of W.H. Smith and John Menzies. Perhaps times are changing again, for *Freedom* and *War Commentary* had occasionally – when enough readers demanded it – a country-wide circulation 'available at all good newsagents'.

Part and parcel of publishing is the news- gathering system. No doubt we can overcome the difficulties, however crippling the bill may be for telephone, postage and distribution.

Next week we shall compose our thoughts on turning on/off lights and drinking water.

22nd July 1995

Now that we are in the midst of cumbersome changes it may be important to examine their effect on the citizen. What better excuse for this model being than when this citizen-client, citizen-customer, ah citizen-consumer, receives his quarterly bill for electricity. Those blessed moments of opening up the envelope, looking at the magic numbers – present 04155, previous 05111 can't be right, how could the citizen have un-used electricity and be charged for 100 units used anyway, converted into pence units. Such are the real joys of life.

Each year the company sends its bills, slightly ever-so unobtrusively altering the terms of supply and charge scales. The model citizen ponders at the collection of bills. Has anything changed in ten years? Not with the citizen's mode of life. The citizen turns on/off the lights with the same regularity as any other anarchist, but unit for unit the payment demand is more. A hundred units (what's that to the national grid?) cost a mere £5.60 in 1985, in 1995 it now costs £8.45. Brilliant, but that's not all.

When John Cage said he was an anarchist, same as you or I, when turning on/off lights, he was not joking. Nevertheless you also have to pay, model citizen, a standing charge. This last phrase means that you pay for hiring their electric meter, which is really an electric motor which turns a rotating disc and the pointers on the dials. Looking at the bill the citizen will also notice that the hiring charge has also gone up in ten years from £7.78 to £13.06. For added amusement there is a new charge compared with 1985: now the citizen will also have to fork out for the greatest insult, a government tax at 8%. All in all the humble citizen within a lapse of ten years is charged double for the same service.

Problems abound. Electricity, like protein, cannot be 'stored' so there is great wastage. Raw materials are burnt uselessly. Because of the nature and the demands of the grid system, large power stations and a network of power lines, with a general insistence of light at all hours of the day and night, have created an economic monster.

Originally electricity was produced when it was needed locally and for local needs. Factories farms and homes generated their own electricity. There was no other cost except maintenance and of installation. Now the model citizen is supplied by a monopoly and pays for units expressed in pence multiplied by kilowatt hours of energy consumed.

Looking ahead to an anarchist society, those who want electricity (candle flame is better for the eyes) will have to pedal for it. The same for the nuclear lobby, for the nuclear industry is really a by-product of electricity generation.

Inhabitants of Mururoa, an island 700 miles south-east of Tahiti and about 400 miles south of the Pitcairn Islands, are also anarchists when they turn on/off their lights. Perhaps a general switch off is needed to stop the tests.

There is now a period of advance, similar to the surge of two centuries ago when Herman Melville was able to write in his *Billy Budd*: "During those years not the wisest could have foreseen that the outcome of [resistance] would result in a political advance along nearly the whole line". There has been, of course, a certain amount of liberation even if the atrocities continue at the expense of the weakest populations. There is no justification whatsoever for the tests, except a word which is usually trotted out in so-called diplomacy – national sovereignty.

It is a long time since the word 'constitutional' has been used for anything else except for jogging. But it is the "constitutional right" of the country pleased to be called France to once more "menace the colourful beauty of Polynesia by the dark cloud of radio-active contamination".

Colony of frogs were found recently by two boys walking by the river. It was a curious find, for most of the frogs had five legs. Guess which industry's waste was pumped into the river which caused this mutation?

S lowly opposition emerges. But it was curious to read in the current *Ethical Record* (always full of interest) a reprint of a talk previously given to the Ethical Society by Chris Busby about the activities of the Green Committee of 100. In the article he makes the astonishing claim that this committee, of whose existence the population is scarcely aware, has effectively initiated and with its members have taken part in *all* the major environmental protect actions and that their members "are now involved in all the direction [sic] action groups". In other words, all the hundreds of activities, occupations, almost the entirety of the marching season, is the doing of this grouping who model themselves on the Wehrmacht (is Chris Busby serious?). Further on in the article he also claims that the "state ought to be proud of all these doings". Citizen-consumer, you have a part to play!

19th August 1995

Summer in England has rarely been so hot. In the metropolis the inhabitants have gone native. The local chemist is full of irate people looking for medicine to cope with the hot weather. A visit to the countryside brings little relief. The fields are parched and the sheep compete with the rabbits for grass. The moles are forced above the ground, the earth is too hard for them to tunnel through.

But the citizens of London make no concessions and do not co-operate. Their million cars pour out their monoxide poison. They show no solidarity with the underground workers and ignore the industrial action.

This is a ruthless, violent society, dehumanised by government, by capitalism, by pressure groups. Atrocities have become commonplace. A local and well-liked man, young and civilised, courteous, was shot in the head by one of Mrs Thatcher's cast-outs. Outside his home tributes of flowers. And a traffic jam. In the country town the same. The houses shake as the juggernauts rattle through the high street past the building where Thomas Paine wrote *Common Sense*. We walk up the hill and look down the valley where the king's army was once defeated.

Radical tradition still flowers here. This was the town that defeated the poll tax. We can still see the local craftswomen at work, this is still an anarchist community. Watching the glassblower fills me with hope. The old skills are still preserved. We need that hot furnace and that gentle skill of blowing through the long pipe shaping a new world. The baby in his mother's arms watches and will remember.

It is not easy to suppress a tear for the young man shot in the head. What a waste of life, what a brutal ending to the life of a marvellous human being. Whom do I must curse? The teachers are at fault. Our rulers, our gun and armament manufacturers, our mentally ill military. At this very moment NATO warplanes are devastating my beloved grandmother's country. And the inheritors of the Revolution of Liberty, Equality and Radioactivity are farting their nuclear bombs into the South Pacific. How can you measure a young man's life against that?

Kropotkin said it in *Act for Yourselves* a hundred years ago: "The words Liberty, Equality and Fraternity are surely grand and glorious words. But what besides the words? Another word? Words painted on prison walls?" On the ground, on the exact spot where the king's army was defeated, there now stands an ugly vast prison.

Authority's revenge, its feeble attempt to erase the truth, to break the spirit of the people. But the king *was* defeated and the walls of that prison will one day come down. We walk to the little island only a dozen miles from the sea. On the hilltop an ancient heap of a church or fortress who can now tell. Red brick pill-boxes left over from the last war. A cow's rump wedged in the entrance. Somewhere in southern England, as the war correspondents used to say so as not to give the exact location away. Loose talk costs life. Hush, Herr Major is listening. This is the last bit of the green belt. Encroached from all sides and parched. Ten years from now it could be a London suburb.

E *arth felt the wound, / and Nature from her seat / Sighing through all her works gave signs of woe / That all was lost,* said Milton. It's down to us, comrades, there is nobody else left except a nine month old child and a brave mother on the barricades. Are we going to stand up for humanity, comrades, or just continue with our forums and talking shops?

9th September 1995

There are many wonderful anarchist sayings which sum up things neatly. One of them is 'Don't ever be fooled by your own propaganda'. The other, which is a bit more devastating, 'Once a thing becomes a success, destroy it', which I took to mean that there is something insincere in repetition. One gets weary repeating the same thing over and over again. After a while one is beginning to talk to the wall. This is the reason that most people just shut up. What's the point of holding onto one's principle? Some mock, some yawn and the majority take no notice.

And what is true in one context becomes untrue in another. And at every juncture there has to be an explanation. It is like the travellers returning from remote regions, their tales of truth are regarded as sheer phantasy. Which is my way of saying that this column has become chapters in a book and it has to be read and understood *in toto* or not at all. It has something to do with a person in the last years of a dying civilisation, a person like it or not who desires to live in anarchy, in an anarchist society, without rulers and masters, without artificial problems. Human existence will never be perfect, but we could do without the constant tripping up by government and vested interest.

This column itself was started on a Scottish island where there were few signs of authority. There were no newspapers and politics were very remote, it was something that took place in the far-off metropolis. Living there was the nearest thing to an anarchist mode of life that I ever experienced. The illusion was furthered that the newspapers were about four days late and after a while I stopped reading them. Authority was practically non-existent and for months I had not seen a policeman or heard the siren either of an ambulance or of the fire brigade. One day a helicopter called to pick up a fisherman who had banged his head on the boom of his vessel. He was lifted up into the sky and was never seen again. There was only one shop in the village and it sold everything from books to tired-looking cabbages.

There was also an inn where the local hooch was sold, and it was vile. In the winter nobody seemed to do a stroke of work but lived on the riches the tourists left behind in the summer. At night you could see the stars and after a while you began to resemble in looks the strange sheep hopping over the fence of your front garden. Once a year, at 'first-footing', the whole village thronged into your parlour and you were violently sick for days from the local whisky pressed on you.

There was no industry except the tourist trade. Some newcomers lived in caravans. The men were fishermen or eked an existence out of the soil. I've not heard politics mentioned or discussed. Each day and night was different. The sea either pounded the coastline or was calm.

There was once a pink granite quarry, but now it lay in the rocks untouched. A few people worked on the ferry or dived for lobsters. The farms were colonised by Christian sects and you avoided them because they gave you the shivers with their candles, sandals and watery blue eyes. Your friends lived in caravans and kept rabbits. It was the slowest of all existences and one day was the same as the next. The water was from the local lake, the colour of brandy.

That's where the idea for this column was born. When you *had* to return to the Big Smoke, at least try to ignore the clamour, the bustle, the violent shoving and still try to lead an anarchist life amongst the vile commerce of the big city.

There was a paradox here which I tried to ignore. For out on those islands they are natural anarchists. Here in the big city, such an animal does not exist. But that does not prove them wrong.

It is lunchtime in the local park. Except for an old man sucking at a bottle, the population is entirely young. Behind the wire fence a ghetto of children in school uniforms kick at balls and shout. Some stand about in groups sharing their thoughts. None of them has a future. I was that child once. The future is of no importance. The sun is shining and the future can wait. By any definition their life in unwanted. They are what they used to call dead-end kids. You can observe them from the outside, that's all you can do.

On my way here I stepped over a man lying flat on the pavement, fast asleep. Perhaps ill, perhaps drunk, perhaps given up life altogether. Perhaps he is dreaming of his childhood. Hanging upside down from a tree, hoping somebody would notice.

23rd September 1995

Fancy that you have received a letter which was once urgent but for some reason or another you have neglected to read. No fault of your own really. You put it somewhere carefully to read it at your leisure, then something else called your attention and by the time you wanted to read it the letter had disappeared.

An annoying, but at least explainable occurrence. Ten years or so later you find the letter which explains everything you wanted to know – but it is a trifle too late. The person who wrote it has gone out of your life – the whole set of people have dispersed, disappeared. Certainly there will be a small satisfaction to realise that what you still hold dear also existed in the past, that your ideas *were* shared by others, that you are not such a maverick after all. At least you hold the letter in your hands and it brings tears to your eyes even though that world is now gone and there is nothing you can do about it. You can't blame anybody else, it was your own fault, your own carelessness.

Recall that Digger once wrote: "There'll always be Chaos, until Anarchy is restored."

Even though, that is nothing compared to what society (if that is the word) can do in making everything that was once important become not only unimportant but completely inaccessible. Technologies change so quickly. Each and every change demands a new apparatus. A few years later you won't find the spare parts, and the whole lot will not work without just that little bit.

What I'm really talking about is anarchism, which needs its own technology, and the unopened letter found ten years later is the best example I can offer at short notice. Yes, the person loved you, *'wait for me'*, the letter said, *'we'll work things out.'* You stare at the letter – you can hardly remember the occasion or even the person who wrote it, the importance of the message is obscured by time. Oh well, it could have been so, it wasn't and now it never will be.

Endlessly the technologies change. Morse-coded telegrams or simple semaphores give way to facsimile transmissions and to multiple digital message packs. The wire tray remains the same, the 'in' is always full, the 'out' is never empty. Life's little pleasures. What is the point of holding on to your superb collection of gramophone records. The gramophone is still there, but you cannot get a stylus. Lovingly you clean and oil the parts and the turntable works perfectly but the needle is worn away, useless. Then ten years later you track down a gloomy person in Tottenham Court Road and this person knows a person who also knows a person who rummages through a box who finds a stylus and *hey presto*, you are able to bring back the true recorded voice of a vanished period. Most of them dead and gone. Every one of them a rebel, a true anarchist. All the people you admire. The shuffled cards of technology have made them all unavailable, except for your treasure trove.

Let it be said, however, that we have been as careful as possible. Anarchist archives are kept at various places, in Amsterdam or at the Bishopsgate Institute to mention only two. Anarchist writings have been kept and annotated with care and attention and nothing much is lost or is irrecoverable (all honour to the VRs and to the NWs) but in other respects little remains of our architectural models, of recipes, of patterns of communication and transport and of modes of exchange.

Laboriously we put things together and in one swipe it all gets shattered. For every time the anarchists (the people, you and I and uncle Tom Cobbley and all) have worked out something simple or something simply brilliant, there come the shuffling bogeymen who change the technology and all our communications are cut and all our children are starving mentally and physically.

Far be it for me to assert that all is lost. Whatever skills human beings possessed in the past, we still possess. But doing cartwheels, either for carts or over our heads, has nowadays become less regarded. A simple set of skis could take you from China to Alaska in winter, and it was a pleasant, safe and exhilarating journey. Today this could only be done on the screen of virtual reality as a simulated existence exercise.

Remarkably we have not lost the capacity to fulfil some simple functions. We can still breathe, eat, walk and blow our noses. But in the past century we have gone into a centrifugal spin when the speed of our answers recurring can no longer compete with the speed of our questions. And never underestimate the obstinate will of the human mind to stay on the treadmill of futility.

Ingeniously we continue with our inventions. This very moment above our heads fly countless numbers of people. Heathrow alone, from dawn to dusk, is a landing space for the arrivals of aircraft at the rate of one a minute. From here to Kathmandu, my loved ones fly as the engine slurps 10,000 gallons of kerosene per journey. You could populate a town the size of Birmingham with the number of people in the air above your distinguished head at this very moment.

Every day and night half of the population traverses the ground on their way to work and back. The rest of the country is deserted, nobody is seen for miles through the car and train windows, the entire population is stuck on long strips of roads and rail, top to tail, cars and lorries, and lorries carrying cars. In each car there is, look in the mirror comrade, an important personage with an unopened letter in a forgotten pocket. An invitation to a dance or an imprint of a lipsticked kiss or the time and date of the revolution from your local LAG (Local Anarchist Group) secretary.

Not to worry. As for me, during the next four hundred hours I'll lock myself in with my record player and will be listening to my 45s, my 78s and to my LPs of Dave Brubeck, Flanders & Swann, The Vipers, David Oistrakh, Under Milk Wood, the Yiddish Anarchist Choir of Pennsylvania and the Twittering Birds of Bucharest. I do not know how these have survived the ravages of time, the oppressors' wrong and the heartless evictions – yet the voice of the turtle is heard throughout the land. But after four hundred hours the stylus is guaranteed to go *kaput, schluss, fini, the end.*

D readful thought. "What happens after that", I asked the man. "After that", he said, "you'd better change your system". "Never", I said, "never". "Don't be a fool, just tape the whole lot and put it onto a compact disc. You can't expect them to make these needles just for you. This is the last of the E419s. Give in, like the rest of them". "Not I", I told him, "Once an anarchist, always an anarchist".

S uch obstinacy is unbecoming to the philosophical mind", he said. "Go digital, that's my advice". "When I need your advice, I'll ask for it". As I left he was still rummaging through his boxes.

7th October 1995

VISIONS OF POESY
AN ANTHOLOGY OF TWENTIETH CENTURY
ANARCHIST POETRY

EDITED BY
CLIFFORD HARPER, DENNIS GOULD and JEFF CLOVES

Seven years in preparation, this eagerly awaited collection is published at a time when popular interest in poetry is at an all time high. The publishers, Freedom Press, believe that *Visions of Poesy* will prove to be a book very much for our times. The editors have chosen over 200 poems from seventy of the best loved poets of this century, all of them committed to an anarchist vision of society. While the poetry in this book spans our entire century, it echoes very strongly the current wave of new poetry. It includes examples of the agitational verse of the Industrial Workers of the World from around 1910, remarkable for its wit and invention, a typical long poem from avant-garde composer John Cage, poems from the '30s and '40s by such poets as Alex Comfort and Herbert Read, the lyrical work of Kenneth Patchen, a wide choice from the Beat poets, including Lawrence Ferlinghetti, Allen Ginsberg and Gary Snyder, a representative selection of post-war English poets, among them Adrian Henri, Bernard Kops, Christopher Logue, Adrian Mitchell, Allan Sillitoe, Stevie Smith and Muriel Spark. The book also contains voices from many of the political causes of recent times, the Vietnam War and the upsurges of the '60s, the feminist wave of the '70s, the anti-nuclear movement and punk. Overall *Visions of Poesy* is informed by an anarchist perspective: all of the poets are or were anarchists. This does not mean that the poetry is simply political and crudely didactic, rather it displays a rejection of the current order combined with a searching for something better.

All of the poetry is in the English language, the book contains no translated work. While the majority of the poets are either English or American, there are many poets from other countries, including Canada, Ireland, Wales, Scotland and New Zealand.

The editors of *Visions of Poesy* have themselves all been deeply involved in both poetry and anarchism for many years. Dennis Gould and Jeff Cloves have been writing and publishing poetry since the mid '60s and have been reading their poetry to appreciative audiences throughout that time. Clifford Harper, an artist and anarchist, has been collecting anarchist poetry for over 25 years.

ISBN 0 900384 75 1   317 pages   £8.00

FREEDOM PRESS
84b Whitechapel High Street, London E1 7QX

ABOUT FREEDOM PRESS

- FREEDOM PRESS are the publishers of the fortnightly journal *Freedom* and of the anarchist quarterly *The Raven*.

- FREEDOM PRESS are the publishers of books and pamphlets on anarchism and allied subjects. Our current list comprises some sixty titles.

- FREEDOM PRESS BOOKSHOP (open Monday to Saturday) carries a comprehensive stock of anarchist literature from this country, the USA and Canada. We also issue lists for the benefit of our mail order customers.

- FREEDOM PRESS DISTRIBUTORS are the European sales representatives for a number of small publishers in this country.

- This book has been printed by ALDGATE PRESS, a successful co-operative venture which also undertakes commercial printing work.

All particulars from
FREEDOM PRESS
84b Whitechapel High Street, London E1 7QX